THREE YEARS IN TENDING

A MEMOIR

Nicholas D. Butler

First Edition
Printed in the United States of America

ISBN 979-8-218-93359-3
Library of Congress Control Number 1-15088791381

Prosaic Publishing
Phoenix, Arizona

@prosaic.publishing

Cover design by @nickbutlerphd
No Artificial Intelligence was used in the composition of this manuscript

In memory of
Sawyer Kenneth Edwards

For anyone who's made a plan;
but decided against it.

3

BEVERAGE LIST

CHAPTER 9
THE SUM OF THE PARTS
rye whiskey ◦ sweet vermouth ◦ cherry

132

CHAPTER 10
THE BARTENDER
pimm's ◦ lemonade ◦ cucumber

214

EPILOGUE
brandy ◦ chocolate liqueur ◦ heavy cream

242

RECOMMENDATIONS
stout ◦ irish cream ◦ vanilla

244

ACKNOWLEDGEMENTS

I'm not a therapist unless you count being a bartender. Self-help books that insist their methods will universally work for readers have always bothered me because they fail to acknowledge their limitations, so let me be clear that I have no idea what works for everyone–I just know what's worked (and failed) for me.

The three years documented in this book were a dark period in my life, but I want everyone who came to my aid to know how much your kindness helped me focus on points of light on the horizon. Whether the act was great or small, I wouldn't be here without your support; so please know how much I value your friendship.

Foremost, Bill Brooks and Richie Black, you gave me room and board when I felt like I had nowhere to go. Without your fellowship during quarantine, I have no idea how I would've survived the pandemic. You're two of the most generous people I've ever met and my heart swells with love thinking about all the laughter we've shared.

Jan Butler and Greg Sanchez, you brought me bags of groceries when I was living hand to mouth and always reminded me that my family was closer than I realized. I couldn't be more happy that you've found companionship in each other and shared your joyous energy with me.

Mike Casley, when the pandemic began, and I was stuck at home desperate for a job, you offered me an opportunity to go to real estate school and join your team. Many people told me they would help me find work, but you were the first to turn those intentions into reality. Thank you for never doubting I could pass some of the toughest tests I've ever faced and always being there for me.

Matt Kuta, thank you for reminding me that my brothers in arms will always be there when needed. Our brainstorming calls and following your advice challenged me in the best possible ways. You're truly an inspiration to me and I'm so proud of the family you've built.

My father, Dale Butler, it's a relief knowing you've found a home in Michigan that's allowed you to finally start enjoying your hard-earned retirement. Thank you for always trusting my decisions knowing that you taught me to make the right choices when faced with difficult decisions.

My mother, Jill Glinsky, you're the glue that holds our Michigan family together, and you deserve nothing but happiness for the way you always find beauty in the overlooked moments of life. Thank you for constantly reminding me of how important it is to communicate. Sarah, Natasha, and I are very fortunate to be your children.

My writing partner, Doug Cunningham, I've never met someone so much like myself. Thank you for graciously forgiving my youth so we can be lifelong friends and pursue our dreams of being filmmakers. I can't wait to see what we're able to create as we continue to collaborate.

Kelly McDonald, no one can empathize with what I've gone through professionally more than you. Your calls are always a bright spot in my week and help me stay the course. Thank you for being Frasier to my Niles. I'm excited for you and Devrie Dimond's new chapter in Tucson!

For better or worse, all my co-workers at Binkley's, Helio Basin, Atlas Bistro, The Whining Pig, as well as Tamara Stanger, Kennan Bosworth, George Murcowicz, Dara Sprinces Wong, Christian Lowe, and everyone I've met in the service industry: You're the hardest working people I've ever met and I truly appreciate the opportunity I've had to learn from you all. The many lessons you taught me over the past several years have completely humbled my perspective and made me a more empathic person.

To all my friends in the beverage community, Dakine Beckman, Jason Wambolt, Jeff Herbert, Bobby Lindeman, Jordan Bartkowiak, Chris Quiroga, Ken Schramm, Ken Weaver, Jon Buford, Katie Buford, Pat Ware, Shay Gau, Ken Schramm, and everyone at The Wandering Tortoise: Thank you for always being as generous in spirit as you are with your pours. You've inspired much more than my writing, but showed me that it's always better to share the finer things in life than keep them to yourself.

To the gay community in Phoenix, Jim Klever, Devina Ross, Barbra Seville, Steven Freed and Jose Martinez: We all need a safe space where we can be ourselves and the four walls of Plazma and NuTowne became that for me. Thank you for always making me feel welcome and having a drink ready. As someone who didn't grow up with examples of other gay men for support, the conversations and stories we've shared mean more to me than you realize.

To the gay community in Palm Springs, Eric Espitia, Greg Devlin, Dan Kitowski, Ric Bills, Tim and Don, Richard and Gerry, Rob McManus, Gary Schneidmiller, and the many friends I've made over the past few years: Spending time with you all is one of the greatest joys I've experienced. Thank you for introducing me to your chosen family that opened my eyes to what happiness looks like when you let go of society's expectations of you and embrace your authentic self.

To my former students and colleagues at ASU, James Qian, Frankie Marchi, Agatha Attridge, Shyam Nair, Michelle Hill, Joe Guffey, Andy Stone, Eddie Gamboa, and anyone who's ever competed in Speech and Debate: Thank you for staying in touch and offering me a window into what's happening in your lives. Social media can be a bleak space, but seeing your accomplishments and continuing to share our brand of Sun Devil humor always brings a smile to my face.

To all of my inspiring friends in NYC, Paul Springs, Elisabeth Weaver, Ken Pace, Paul Marlow, Joshua Sanchez, and T. Cole Rachel: Thank you for showing me that anything is possible in The City. What you've accomplished professionally and creatively drives me to try and catch up. Spending time with you is always a treat and there's a part of me that suspects we'll be neighbors at some point in my career.

Mort Scult and the Sagewood Retirement Community, lecturing over the past decade to a group of hundreds of seniors who've lived incredible lives is a daunting task that I'm proud you've encouraged me to embrace. Thank you for listening to my thoughts on cinema and engaging me in some of the best conversations I've ever had. Our Zoom meetings during quarantine gave me a healthy outlet and reassured me that we would collectively find a way through the pandemic.

My IFA Family, Jim Dobson, Michael McHan, Sarah Hinkle, Tomeka Robinson, Sondera Malry, Gloria Batiste-Roberts, Jill Kraatz, and everyone who's traveled abroad with the organization: Thank you for believing in my leadership and for all of the sacrifices you've made to enable the speech and debate community to engage new cultures and ideas through travel and competition. I truly believe that we've changed thousands of lives for the better and my time as President was one of the great honors of my career in forensics.

My high school teachers and lifelong guardians, Carole and John Robert, it's hard to believe I'm in my 40s now and you've watched over me for more than half of those years. Thank you for always being patient with me as a precocious person and reminding me that the best parts of me have stayed the same. Whenever I'm lost, your advice guides me in the right direction.

Finally, Virginia Cavelletti, Matt Gjertsen, Quincy Conley, and everyone who helped me leverage my professional network to find my new job as a consultant: Thank you for believing in my potential to find fulfilling labor outside of higher education. One of the biggest mistakes I ever made was shackling my identity to a profession instead of embracing the many opportunities life has to offer. I'm excited for the journey ahead and proud to be able to compose this work as a means of expressing my gratitude.

PROLOGUE

CLINIC INTAKE FORM

3 January 2020

Are you currently having any of the following problems?

Feelings of depression?   [Yes]

Loss of interest in activities?   [Yes]

Feeling hopeless?   [Yes]

Problems going to sleep?   [Yes]

Racing thoughts?   [Yes]

Acting impulsively?   [Yes]

Worrying excessively?   [Yes]

Feeling worthless?   [Yes]

Traumas that come back in nightmares?   [Yes]

Feeling awkward in public?   [Yes]

Having tense muscles?   [Yes]

Repetitive or compulsive behaviors?   [Yes]

Thoughts that replay?   [Yes]

Eating too little?   [Yes]

Concerns about alcohol use?   [Yes]

Problems caring for yourself?   [Yes]

Thoughts of not being alive?   [   ]

STAGE 1
PRE-CONTEMPLATION

People who are in the first stage of recovery aren't yet ready for any treatment program. This phase is characterized by defensiveness and endless justification of their behavior.

Someone might remain in this stage due to a lack of information about addictive behaviors. Another reason we regularly see people get stuck in the pre-contemplation stage is disappointment with multiple failed attempts at recovery and treatment options.

Most individuals in pre-contemplation feel that recovery simply isn't possible for them. The truth is that anyone can recover from any stage.

17

CHAPTER 1

THE BOTTOM OF THE BOTTLE

I started bartending when I could see the bottom of the bottle in my hand and was confronted with whether to have another round or leave. Not to go home, but to place a letter I'd written outlining instructions for my burial and an explanation for my decision on the kitchen counter, then quietly go outside to sink to the bottom of our pool with a belly full of pills. That was the choice my mind repeatedly cycled over like a washing machine on a nightly basis for months while it took me hours to fall asleep.

After a year of working in a restaurant that cared more about its bottom line than the intense stress the job mentally, physically, and emotionally demanded of its staff, it was painfully clear that the abusive pattern was unsustainable. I was drinking heavily after shifts to cope with the pressure and numb my frustrations. On a nightly basis samples of beer and wine at work would lead to spirits at home that inevitably led to doubles until I passed out. The effect was like drowning in my surroundings, and I was desperately trying to find a way to stay afloat.

To further complicate the issue, my retired husband spent the day drinking gin until they passed out or provoked an argument, so there wasn't any refuge at home. My friends were busy raising children and facing their own challenges, so reaching out to them seemed selfish. My family had always been a source of pride, so asking for support felt embarrassing. I needed help, but from whom?

I've always insisted on helping myself and bought into the misguided idea of suffering in silence and pulling myself up by the bootstraps. After all, that's how society expects people–especially veterans like myself–to shoulder their burdens. I'd been to therapy several times over the years, most recently in marriage counseling, but never found that talking through the psychology of issues was enough. Being thoughtful generally isn't one of my problems–it's anxiously overthinking. The older I've grown, the more I've realized that a significant part of the problems I've struggled with are as much biochemical as behavioral, so the first step I took toward recovery was seeking help from a psychiatrist.

While there are hotlines for mental health and support organizations that are ready to assist in times of emergency, making an appointment with a psychiatrist can take months. Moreover, the demand is apparently so high for mental health treatment that there aren't enough doctors to go around. Waiting two months wasn't an option in my situation, so the best option I could find was a methadone clinic where intake counseling was provided to receive a prescription.

The intake room was packed with people, largely staring into their cell phones, with a few manically pacing around muttering to themselves. A security guard monitored the room and turned away anyone who came to the door clearly under the influence. My mental health had reached a point of desperation on par with trying to recover from drug addiction.

When a nurse practitioner was finally able to see me, she reviewed the intake form and the first question she asked was, "Do you have a plan?"

"Like a five year plan?" I replied.

The nurse just stared back until I realized she was asking if I had reached the point of planning my suicide.

I could only answer by shaking my head before emotionally breaking down in tears. It was the first time I'd admitted my state of mind to someone. I needed help, but the only person I was able to open up to was a stranger. She wasn't able to write a prescription for my anxiety, but she suggested I use passion flower essential oil to help me go to sleep. I knew that wouldn't help. What I needed was a referral to someone who could assist me for the long-term instead of rushing me through a process.

Applying for jobs in the 9 to 5 world had become an exercise in futility by hurling applications into a black hole, so the allure of sidestepping the entire process by staying in the service industry became the only short-term option for staying employed. Teaching had never provided enough to cover a mortgage and expenses, so side work in the service industry had become a means to an end. Many people look down on bartending, but it's an honest trade. Unless your dream is to be a mixologist, it's a fairly straightforward job: pour drinks and try to manage a smile. We transport beverages to guests, and they hypothetically tip us for doing the task for minimum wage. It's a job that rarely comes with benefits, much less stability, but is always hiring.

In my case, the opportunity came in the form of a social media post from a friend looking for bartenders at their nearby brewery. I sent a private message, met up the next day, and was covering shifts pouring drinks by the end of the week. The focus was on beer, but we also served wine and made house cocktails. We served food, but nothing compared to working in fine dining. Pub fare offered a welcome respite from the intensity of trying to host the perfect dinner on a nightly basis. Taking orders that simply require asking which sides, dressings, and cheese a guest prefers is a largely predictable interaction that doesn't require too much of a challenge. The change in scenery helped me realize that finding a role with dramatically less stress involved was a necessary step toward recovery.

The brewery was a sprawling open space with a vast, two-story, glass enclosure shielding all the towering equipment in the rear of the property. The horseshoe-shaped bar was situated in the center of the room in front of the swinging doors to the kitchen with a view facing the front door to greet guests. There were two televisions on either side of the bar playing sports, and games like foosball were scattered across the facility. The atmosphere was relaxed and proved a welcome change in pace from dining. Even so, when you're still tending to other people's wants, it doesn't leave much for your own needs.

Unfortunately, my marriage continued to deteriorate due to my continuing late shifts as well as our sustained drinking. The only short-term solution I could think of was to stop drinking hard alcohol to gradually help us lower our intake, but my husband's daily habits had already become a dependency. We were enabling each other and in denial about what needed to happen—our imminent separation.

I didn't know where to go when I ultimately left my marriage, so I found a room on AirBnB to give me a few days to find a place to live. Housing, particularly rental properties, were and continue to be scarce in the Phoenix metro area. I would search online and go to visit a property only to find that it had been rented hours after it became available. My time and money on a bartender's wages were quickly running out. Thankfully, two of my friends offered me a room to stay in for a week while I continued my search. Eventually, I found a place with a studio apartment that was still available when I arrived for a tour. While speaking to the property manager they noted that a one-bedroom unit had become available that morning, so I pounced on the opportunity sight unseen.

It turned out that the apartment was in a corner on the top floor of a four-story, block-construction building from the 50s that proved to be shockingly quiet for a location in the heart of the city only a mile away from the brewery. The downside was an absence of air conditioning, particularly as the summer months were closing in, but I figured I could stand the heat as long as I finally had a place of my own to dry up and make sense of the direction I was headed in.

Unfortunately, the abused shared spaces in the complex, routine police presence, incessant noise, and perpetually broken facilities regularly made me question the decision. People would smoke cigarettes on the elevator and occasionally there would be the added bonus of a puddle of urine in one of the corners to greet me on the way home. Booming hip-hop music provided a soundtrack for residents that seemed to dare anyone to make a noise complaint. A woman would frequently scream in the evenings as if she were starring in a Hitchcock film, and public arguments similarly intensified in volume to the point of security interventions.

By the time COVID had escalated to a point of requiring quarantine, I was completely alone in my surroundings. It felt like my door was a barricade against the rapidly spreading virus. Was it in the hallways? Were other residents infected? How was it being transmitted? The fears of hospitalization and potentially death were overwhelming. Inside my apartment felt like the only safe place. Being cut off from the outside world as well as my drinking habits gave me a place to lick my wounds and recover from hitting bottom.

Writing allowed my mind to stay active. The silence proved deafening to the thoughts processing in my mind. Rewatching my favorite movies was a welcome escape. It was a reminder of better times and normalcy. The thought of being in a theater with friends and crowds suddenly seemed like that might never happen again. What would the films of the future look like as society continued to fracture?

After the first week of quarantine I began a routine of walking along a nearby canal for exercise as well as an opportunity to clear my head. Walking outside with no one else felt like surviving a post-apocalyptic event. I was living on one of the busiest streets in Phoenix and could look in all four directions at an intersection without seeing a single car on the road. It was like in *Home Alone* waking up to your family having vanished. People were disappearing.

My great aunt and uncle were the first I personally knew who succumbed to the virus. Married for over 50 years, they died in separate rooms. I couldn't help but consider how my husband and I would've fared under the same circumstances. Would we spend our waning moments communicating through glass and take peace in passing on together? The parallel to the HIV/AIDS crisis began to materialize in my thoughts. Is this what it must have felt like to see your community decay from infection? Would there be a strange relief in knowing you were joining the fate of those you loved by contracting the virus? What measures would it take to avoid becoming a victim?

If I didn't survive, one way or another, would my life in some way live on through what had been documented in my work? Had I written too little or more than anyone cared to follow? In the age of social media and digital presence, what had meant the most to me that warranted sharing? People measure their lives in many ways, but almost always through a form of comparison. Did I achieve more than my parents, my peers, and even myself ever thought? I don't think so. What truly mattered in the long view?

Meanwhile, the final days of the brewery paralleled the ending of my marriage. We'd tried last ditch efforts to sell drinks to go as a stopgap, but no one was coming in. I'd stand for hours pacing behind the bar looking for things to do. Still unaware of how the virus was spread we took out half the chairs and spaced them more than six feet from each other. The place was covered in caution tape like a crime scene, and I fixated on cleaning up the evidence of anyone's presence. The shifts grew so boring that one day I took apart the popcorn machine down to the last screw before reassembling it just to bide the time.

I knew there was no way to continue paying me to tend to a bar without patrons, so I braced myself for being out of work for the first time in my life. On my final day at the brewery I made a single dollar as a tip. At that point I knew there was no hope of bartending during the surge in COVID, so I grudgingly began to accept the government-subsidized unemployment checks to get by financially.

By the time businesses began to reopen, the brewery had closed and sold to a more popular brand that saw a spike in business due to the demand for takeout during the pandemic. Small businesses closed and larger corporations received Payroll Protection loans they largely never repaid. Free money for the rich and a stimulus check for the struggling poor who lost their service industry jobs was a hard truth to face in returning to the workforce.

However, like the brewery owners, the truth is that in hitting bottom we accepted that there were ways to move on. I knew that my drinking had gone too far, my professional choices had dramatically shifted the trajectory of my career, and my mental health was in a state of dark depression. Tending to others before myself had led to a pattern of self-destruction. It was easy to place blame on others for the role they played in my struggles, but as the distance grew between us I slowly began to realize that I was the only person who could put down the metaphorical bottle in my hand in order to pick myself back up.

27

CHAPTER 2

DIVORCE IN THE TIME
OF SOCIAL DISTANCING

My marriage reached terminal condition during the era of "social distancing." While the late hours that bartending required contributed to the diagnosis, there were deep-seated problems with our relationship long before the world literally went viral. After 15 years together, our partnership started to feel like a sickness we couldn't recover from. The symptoms were undeniable. We'd tried counseling, exotic vacations, extravagant dining experiences, and nothing seemed to provide a cure. The physical and emotional distance between us was growing further by the day, so the decision to separate was the only healthy way to protect each of our futures as well as those surrounding us from tragedy. The world was dying and so were we.

On March 1st, I sent a formal letter to dozens of universities and colleges as the President of the International Forensics Association to make a public announcement that the 30th Anniversary of our annual speech and debate tournament slated for the following week in Tokyo would have to be canceled for reasons that have now become obvious but at the time seemed controversial. Like major sporting events that were indefinitely postponed at the last minute, we were the first tournament of our kind to follow suit. There were hundreds of students and dozens of coaches that still wanted to travel to compete despite the health warnings, but we all knew that ensuring the safety of everyone involved was far more important than any tournament.

It was one of the most difficult decisions I've ever had to make. I say that not because of the overwhelming amount of data we analyzed or the many conversations concerning the ethics involved, but because planning the event for years and looking forward to seeing all the participants have the experience of a lifetime was one of the only thoughts that kept me alive through months of depression. When that marker on the calendar was erased, I was left with nothing to look forward to but my next bartending shift.

At the time, I was teaching online part-time and bartending for tips after spending the previous year working in fine dining for minimum wage. I was desperate for long-term employment and a sustainable career path. Years before, I left my commission as an officer in the military because I couldn't be with my husband due to the "Don't Ask, Don't Tell" policy of the era. I gave up on my dream of becoming a filmmaker because my husband judged that it was impractical, and I quit an incredible role teaching in Europe to return to Arizona so he could wait for a liver transplant.

Meanwhile, my husband (25 years my senior) maintained the stability he demanded to enjoy the level of comfort provided by continuing his long-standing tenure as a professor as well as running a lucrative side business as the owner of an art gallery. Marriage requires sacrifice, but I wouldn't recommend taking it to the lengths I went to for my spouse. One of the most important lessons my marriage and the era of social distancing taught me is that no one's life, even with the best of intentions and abundance of love, is meant to be lived in service to someone else.

Those around us, much like relatives who continued to gather in groups and friends not exercising precautions in public during the pandemic, might disagree with me on the subject of sacrifice and their perception of our marriage. Yet, as a 40-year old veteran who graduated from a world-class service academy, earned a Ph.D. from a Research 1 university, and sacrificed 15 years of my life for a person I dearly love; I can attest that no level of public accomplishment can replace the necessity of personal satisfaction. As I now realize, no one, even my partner, could provide that type of fulfillment for me except myself.

People talk about balance in relationships, but from my experience that's rarely possible. Whether you're in anything from bed to business with another person an exchange is taking place and it's rarely equitable. Our society perpetuates a culture of sacrifice in relationships that exploits selflessness. For example, I volunteered the formative years of my life to the military, and now I get a 10% discount on Veterans Day.

My first intimate relationship with another gay man started when I was 22 and lasted until the week the pandemic began to spread in the United States, so I've been socially distant from other people I identify with for the first half of my life. I'm an award-winning educator who's coached several students to national championships in public speaking contests, but the only job opportunities available to me in higher education are part-time or "adjunct" positions that senior faculty abuse for wildly disproportionate salaries. Younger generations are always expected to sacrifice their future for the older generation's present. In turn, I've come to the realization that I've been taken advantage of by my partner, my profession, and even my country. So, where do I, and anyone who identifies with my story, go from here? Is the choice truly between stoic isolation or exploitation in the marketplace?

It's been over three years since I've been separated from my husband and I still don't know the answer to those questions. The details of our divorce were coordinated digitally through lawyers while our marriage was quarantined. During that time, I woke up alone in my one-bedroom apartment while my ex stayed in our home with our pets. I applied for job postings with hundreds of other applicants while he was able to transition to teaching online from home. I ate a single meal a day to save money while his diet stayed the same. I took long walks to meditate on my situation while he remained sedentary on the couch. I wrote as truthfully as I could to process our collective grief while he read the newspaper.

By the time the period of COVID drew to a conclusion and we officially divorced I realized I'd voluntarily played the role of the loser in our marriage. I always gave when asked and never spoke up to ask for the same. Unable to break the pattern of sacrifice during the negotiation of our settlement, I left with a fraction of what I was financially entitled to because I'd always accepted less. Moving forward, I resolved to quit placing others' wants before my own needs.

When I think about the future, I try to envision my former husband retiring to a comfortable apartment, maybe in New York, where he can walk to all the inspiring museums and indulge in all the Broadway productions that his heart desires. I hope he sleeps in and takes his time reading the newspaper with our dog cuddled on their lap. I pray that he enjoys the remaining days of his life, however distant we've grown, and let the brighter memories we shared outshine the gloom of our struggles. Should he fall in love again, which I wish he does, I hope it's with someone he'll treat more as an equal rather than the way he treated me. After all, on the other side of this period of time to reconsider our civilization,

I hope everyone will agree that balance is the antidote we all deserve from both our personal and professional relationships. Life is too short to accept anything less.

STAGE 2
CONTEMPLATION

Even if a person is struggling to understand the root of their problems and how to recover, simply thinking about potential courses of action to take is a gigantic step forward.

During this phase, contemplators report increased feelings of hopelessness, but these are often combatted by uplifting feelings of potential for change. Once a person shifts more into thinking about the future rather than lingering on their past, they will be ready to move into the next stage of recovery.

People nearing the end of this stage often say that they no longer feel "hopeless." Instead, those feelings are replaced by simultaneous excitement and anxiety.

CHAPTER 3

THE GLASS IS HALF EMPTY

I've been in denial about my mental health for the majority of my life. Growing up in the military community, the subject was even more taboo than talking about sex in the era of the "Don't Ask, Don't Tell" policy that threatened the dishonorable discharge of soldiers like myself for homosexual conduct. I knew I was different from most kids in school, but when you're young you don't know anything other than your surroundings and what you're taught. You get called names, but you try not to take them seriously. When they call you a *faggot* because your voice is still high while everyone's going through puberty, you start to silence your expression. When they call you a *pussy* because you're smaller and don't have many friends, you start to avoid conflict. When they call you *retarded* because you have trouble fitting in socially, you start thinking they might be right. By the time you're an adult, you realize you've been conditioned to keep your problems to yourself by the very people who've created them for you.

The persistent stress of working in the service industry at mid-life brought back the worst memories of my upbringing. Counting and aligning everything to exacting measures brought out my obsessive-compulsive tendencies. Interacting with guests at the bar grated on my anxiety. Minor mistakes like forgetting to fill a water glass haunted me for days. The intensity of meeting precise standards and routinely being barked at brought back trauma from being in the military. My dreams, when I had enough sleep to have them, turned into nightmares of drowning under the pressure. My mood grew more erratic because the slightest hint of disrespect would set me off and stoke the codependent issues that have ruined far too many of my friendships.

Ultimately, the cocktail of high expectations, demanding guests, and self-imposed pressure initiated a long period of depression with regular thoughts of ending my life to silence the pain. Acknowledging these conditions was the first step in trying to be more mindful about my behavior and developing an ability to manage the pressing mental-health issues I was dealing with following months of unemployment during the pandemic and a divorce that spanned a year and a half.

Returning to bartending as businesses slowly reopened signaled the end of introspection and the start of a period of contemplation. I needed to find out whether it's possible to find a sustainable way to succeed in the world of hospitality without carrying the weight of your personal issues to work. The following sections wrestle with tracing the roots of these problems and connecting them to triggering aspects of working in the service industry:

Anxiety

The worst part of being a bartender is the unpredictability of dealing with guests. The moments between greeting someone as they walk in and leaving them feeling like they've enjoyed themselves are fraught with questioning your phrasing, worrying whether they like you, and hoping to avoid any conflict. It seems so easy to think you're simply transporting liquid from one vessel to another, but it's the human element that complicates the task. Will they ask for something I don't know how to make? What if I forget their order? How will I carry all of these glasses at once? Most people don't care, but that's where my mind gravitates toward a place of worry. In short, I have a fear of disappointing guests that largely stems from not wanting people to dislike me or think that I'm somehow failing my own high standards.

○ ○ ○

I was raised as an only child with a single father in the military. He and my mother married in their early 20s and divorced at an age where I was too young to understand what was happening. My first memory is of being on one side of a barrier to keep toddlers contained to a safe space while my parents argued like a war happening in our own home.

To complicate matters, my father joined the Air Force and the decision was made that I would live with him in another country on the other side of the world in Japan. Their separation led to a fear of abandonment I've held on to throughout my life. I learned at an early age that your surroundings can change with little to short notice no matter how much you wish for them to stay the same. Everyone will eventually leave. Unlike many of my peers, my upbringing was spent on the move with my father while sharing the summers with my mother, who later joined the Army. Stability was something I wouldn't find until I finally left the military after my own service.

As a result, my anxiety would peak in times of transition. One of the earliest examples I can recall is when my father had to leave on a temporary duty assignment overseas to Egypt. It was around the time of the Gulf War in the early 90s and required my father to leave me behind to be looked after by neighbors. During his absence I began to feel intense pain in my stomach; something in retrospect I associate with having a psychosomatic event. I was in the hospital for a significant period of time to the point where I was slow to return to walking, but the doctors could never figure out why I was feeling such agony—even after conducting what they called "exploratory surgery" on my stomach leaving a scar the length of my abdomen that I've been marked by ever since.

Moreover, at some point in my youth I started doing things like chewing on pencils in class and licking my lips out of anxiety. It got to the point where I would regularly chew the metal and eraser off a pencil and my lips would be chapped for days. I looked like a clown and heard as much from the kids at school. The more they made fun of me, the more anxious I grew about what people were thinking and the chewing and licking continued. I can't pinpoint how I finally stopped, but becoming conscientious of when I was doing either was certainly a key. It's like stopping someone from saying "like" in public speaking. You don't realize you're doing it until someone points it out or you see a recording of yourself. Then it becomes about actively trying to stop the behavior.

By the time I started high school the habit had faded, but going through Basic Cadet Training at the U.S. Air Force Academy for my freshman year of college took my anxiety to an exponential level. The year-long indoctrination process is designed to push your mind, body, and spirit to a breaking point, so every day was exhausting. In order to survive, I needed a place where I felt some level of security and I found it in the most unlikely of spaces: the speech and debate community.

Sports were usually the way I fit in. I was socially awkward, but athletically gifted, so teammates generally welcomed me. It was a way to quickly try and make friends when we moved to a new place, so being a jock became my tribe. However, once I made it to a Division I university, I was suddenly an average player at that level. In turn, the sports I was best at like distance running and soccer were no longer options for me to seek support by joining a team.

By happenstance, I went to a club day where booths were set up for all the different activities beyond athletics. One of the things I excelled at the most academically was doing presentations; not because I felt comfortable–quite the opposite–but because I loved the creativity in approaching assignments from a different perspective. So when I saw one of the booths set up with a television showing students giving speeches, I stopped by to inquire about joining their team. They took down my email and a few days later I was invited to audition at practice.

I immediately felt like I was in over my head and nearly avoided the opportunity altogether, but something inside me responded to the challenge of doing a task that terrifies the average person: public speaking. I wanted to have the feeling of being valued by a team outside of sports and this was my chance.

When I arrived at practice, the senior cadets were organizing pairings for a round of debates–something I had never done before. Again, my anxiety skyrocketed because I was expecting to give a speech, but was suddenly thrown into defending an issue I knew virtually nothing about. Plus, I had no idea how to follow all the rules and decorum that were expected in an official debate contest. Suddenly, I felt myself beginning to lick my lips again. Why was I the only person who was struggling like this?

I clearly wasn't a natural or skilled debater, but what saved me from humiliation was a form of comedy I had learned to use as a coping mechanism: self-deprecating humor. It was plain to see that I was unskilled at the nuances of debate, but what I brought to the team was an ability to make a joke out of an awkward situation in an entertaining way. They thought I was *funny* enough to welcome me into their fold, and the people pleaser inside me was grateful for being accepted.

Stress

Bartending can be as difficult as you want it to be. Working in the service industry created an entirely new set of expectations I internally placed on myself in order to treat customers the way I'd like to be treated. Personally, I believe that every guest should be warmly greeted, have their questions answered with patience, and served promptly. My goal is always to anticipate guest needs and help them feel welcome. When I enter a business, I hate not being acknowledged, having my questions brushed off, and waiting an unreasonable amount of time. Not doing this for everyone who walks through the door is a failure to me, so it can quickly become stressful when you get too busy to give everyone the time they deserve. You can never tell how busy you'll be. There's the financial stress of not knowing if your paycheck will be enough for the week when it's slow, the physical stress on your body of moving rapidly for hours when you're making money, and the emotional stress that comes from trying to please everyone.

○ ○ ○

It all starts with whether you care about your work, and I care way too much. My parents never placed any pressure on me to perform at the highest level in any of my pursuits, but my coaches and teachers always challenged me to do my best in order to reach my potential. In turn, the major source of my stress as an anxious person has always been meeting (if not exceeding) people's expectations.

My perception as an adolescent was that falling short of expectations or letting someone down wasn't an option in terms of my family and community's values. If you say you're going to do something then you should perform the task as well as you can. Period. Avoidance or making excuses aren't unacceptable outcomes, so I've always placed high expectations (and in turn stress) on myself.

In particular, the social pressure to go to college or be considered a failure was the driving force behind my focus academically. I can recall numerous times when I was taken aside by teachers for freaking out about my grades, and it's a behavior I've seen echoed in students throughout my teaching career. The fear of letting someone down is a powerful form of motivation that often leads to ignoring your own instincts and desires.

For example, I applied to two types of universities: military service academies and liberal arts colleges. The former to prove to my family and friends that I could graduate from one of the most challenging experiences in the world, and the latter to move to an environment that would cultivate my love of the humanities. When forced to make a decision between the two, I predictably chose the most difficult option; which gratefully carried the least financial burden for my parents and me. Worrying about whether my grades and test scores were good enough to go to school weighed heavily on me, as I didn't know how we could afford tuition to a private college, so I took on the self-imposed responsibility of going to a place I knew would never make me happy.

Similarly, the hospitality industry is rife with depression from unfulfilling labor. In my experience, bartenders generally take pride in their work, but don't take an interest in the long-term reputation of a bar because they're rarely netting more than minimum wage and tips.

After all, it's a transient business and change is constantly occurring as bartenders leave and are inevitably replaced by someone who needs the job. Given the option, most people would choose the place with the least amount of stress, so for one of the first times in my life I chose to lower my expectations.

Anger

My greatest challenge as a bartender is controlling my temper. I don't think guests intentionally behave in abusive ways, but there are few things that infuriate me more than people being oblivious to how their conduct affects those around them. In the service industry, it's always the management or the guests that will get under your skin. You expect people to behave with civility, but the ones that do are in the minority. You expect management to care, and they rarely do. You expect other bartenders to communicate, but they don't. The frustration builds until you lose your composure and remains until you eventually quit.

○ ○ ○

My father has always been hard on himself, and I know part of the way I deal with stress is modeled on how rapidly his mood could change when things didn't go the way he planned or the way he thought they should. Life rarely follows a rational path; particularly when dealing with people, so when things go sideways it can be hard to maintain a level of calm. I can recall my father's aggression that could instantly turn on a single comment or action. Even going to the movies was intense because everything the other audience members were doing would grate at him like nails on a chalkboard. The first time I knew my father was more angry than most people was when I heard adults start using the phrase "short fuse" as if he could explode at any moment.

According to my parents, I had colic that made me cry for hours at a time as a child. Later, that same behavior manifested in moments as a teenager where I became so overwhelmed with anger out of frustration I'd find an empty room to scream in. Why such frustration at an early age? I'm sure there are genetic markers that influence my temperament beyond my control, but my anger is also rooted in accepting that my life hasn't turned out the way I hoped it would. I've been let down innumerable times.

Perhaps the most painful disappointment was when my former step-mother left my father. At the time, he was in the process of setting up housing for us at his next duty assignment in Germany while I finished my last semester of middle school. I was already anxious about having to leave my friends and start high school in a completely new country, but I never expected that my step-mother would pick me up from school in a brand new white Mustang to tell me that she was leaving us. I can recall how she took me to a shop for sports collectibles to let me pick something out to soften the news, but the anger I felt didn't want anything from her other than distance–much less a memento that would remind me of her betrayal. She drove home and abandoned me to find a friend to stay with until my father flew home. That was the last time I ever saw her.

A person's word means a lot to me, so it's hard to accept behavior that avoids or rejects this value. I'm often told not to have expectations of others, and it always frustrates me. I view it as an excuse for people like my step-mother not to be accountable even when they make a vow. It infuriates me beyond control because I view it as a double-standard. After all, why shouldn't I expect you to do what you said you would do? Should I not trust anyone?

Trauma

You see some crazy things when bartending. Guests are an unpredictable variable, and when you add alcohol to the equation the algebra can get messier than fractions. Guests black out and confuse the bathroom sink for the toilet when they throw up. Junkies shoot up and pass out by the dumpster. People living on the street and struggling with mental illness burst in at all times of day. Every shift has the potential for becoming another story, but also carries a certain amount of risk that other professions never have to consider.

Long hours on your feet take a toll on your body and taking medication like opioids to numb the pain can lead bartenders to a path of addiction. Staying open until the early hours of the next day alone with a single patron or two feeds an anxiety associated with the unknown of what might happen without witnesses. And then, of course, is the inevitable news that yet another coworker in the industry has overdosed or committed suicide. The longer you stay in, the longer the list of those lost grows. It's an embedded trauma in the community that comes with the territory. For example, when I started working in fine dining our sous chef was fired for alcoholism and a chef friend at another restaurant died of alcohol poisoning in the first month. The news was so commonplace that long-term workers basically shrugged and said, "That's a shame," before going back to business as usual. It doesn't take much time to realize how disposable you are to the business of tending to others rather than yourself.

○ ○ ○

My upbringing largely avoided trauma, but that all changed when I joined the military. In college, on a team of approximately 20 speech and debate students, both of my debate partners died from vehicle crashes. It was sobering because when they tell you in college that if you look to your left and right, at least one of the people next to you will be gone by the time you graduate. The comment is meant to address academic or emotional attrition, but my situation was about survival. Not unlike bartending, being in the military puts you at higher risk.

Once I was commissioned as an officer in the military, one of my first duties as an officer was commanding the honor guard that provided funeral ceremonies to veterans. It was the hardest job I've ever had because of the emotional weight of looking in parents' and spouses' eyes to thank them for their loved one's service. I performed dozens of ceremonies where I presented the flag to those in mourning, and it never got easier. The worst part of the detail was when families blamed the military, and I became the symbolic figure for their loss. I was barely 21 at the time and ill-equipped to handle that type of profound disappointment, so the period lives in my memory as a source of trauma.

Borderline Tendencies

Bartenders always have something to say and the good ones know when to keep it to themselves. I struggle with the latter. If you're sarcastic to me, then I'm going to have a sarcastic reply. If you're positive, then we'll get along great. If you're negative, then we're going to have a problem.

To me it's all about civility, and when someone isn't respectful it's hard for me not to speak up.

I've always had intense feelings of inevitable abandonment that undermine relationships, dramatic mood swings that feel uncontrollable, and an inability to filter the way I express my thoughts–all symptoms of Borderline Personality Disorder. My feelings about a person or issue can change in an instant and often have negative long-term repercussions. In short, I've lost a lot of friends and gained a number of enemies over the years. It's hard for me to let go of things like perceived disrespect. Behind the bar, a snide comment from someone would alter my mood for an entire shift.

○ ○ ○

I've always been outspoken, if not downright obnoxious. It's something that's taken the better part of a lifetime to curb and I still struggle with respecting sources of authority who'd much prefer I stay quiet. Going back to my elementary report cards, the teacher feedback section would consistently say things like "disruptive in class" and "inappropriate behavior" that can generally be summarized as being insubordinate or exceptionally precocious. I can recall a moment in the 5th grade when my teacher grew so frustrated with me that she actually picked me up and dumped me into the class's garbage can. Similarly, in many of my middle school classes I'd be directed to sit at a desk that faced the corner so I'd be less distracting to the other students.

As I grew older and started puberty my mood swings became more difficult to control and relationships became exponentially more complicated when I began feeling attracted to other people. I had flirtations with girls in high school and college, but never a girlfriend. I can recall going to prom with one of my best friends and struggling to even muster the courage to kiss. Competing for women's attention simply hasn't been a priority for me. Testosterone didn't spike in my veins the way it did for most of the other boys in high school, but that's not to say that my interests detoured from the masculine. Quite the opposite, I joined the Junior Reserve Officer Training Corps (JROTC), played a different sport every season, and my circle of friends was virtually all male. I started reading Hemingway, studying Freud, and subscribing to magazines like GQ and Esquire. It took me years to understand that my behavior was overcompensating for a fear of being exposed as gay and rejected by my community.

During this period, an unhealthy pattern emerged in my friendships and romantic interests: quickly become infatuated with someone, unconsciously overwhelm them with attention, and inevitably turn sour when the feeling is unrequited. The first time I can recall this happening was when I started high school and joined JROTC. I know I joined to show everyone that I was willing to serve in the military like my parents, but I committed to becoming one of the best cadets the school had ever seen for a much different subconscious reason.

The instructor was a retired Lieutenant Colonel with silver hair and looks like my favorite actor, Cary Grant. I had no idea why I couldn't keep my eyes off of the instructor like being transfixed by a film. The infatuation grew into spending the majority of my free time volunteering for events and generally doing anything I could to hold his attention. In turn, over the next four years I went on to earn a chest of medals that made me look like a member of the Joint Chiefs of Staff. Meanwhile, I can only imagine how inappropriate my behavior became for the instructor as I pushed his boundaries in every direction.

Our breaking point came in my senior year when applying to colleges and he wrote what I perceived as a negative letter of recommendation. Perhaps he knew why I'd fixated on him long before I ever understood and he tried to protect me from the hardship of discovering my sexuality was punishable by a dishonorable discharge if I joined the military. Regardless, in my eyes it was a betrayal I couldn't forgive and foreshadowed the way I'd painfully break away from anyone who'd reject or ignore my advances for decades to come. I knew (or at least felt) I'd inevitably be left, so my defense mechanism became to test the limits of someone's connection to a point of choosing between bonding or separating.

Obsessive Compulsion

Beyond my interpersonal relationships with coworkers and guests behind the bar, working in the service industry made my obsessive tendencies go off the charts. Everything was fussed over and counted to achieve perfection. The spacing of silverware and the position of chairs were all aligned symmetrically. Cocktails had exacting measurements and cleaning was always happening. There's a "proper" way of accomplishing a task in any business, and it all depends on the culture of the establishment.

○ ○ ○

Personally, I've always felt better when everything is in its right place and under control. My grandmother used to obsessively clean everything on a daily basis like scrubbing down a professional kitchen, so I suppose I get it in part from her side of the family, but my father also has an exacting eye for spotting imperfections that's been passed on to me. It's difficult not to fix or adjust something once I notice it's broken or out of place, and there's not much that I miss. It's a gift and a curse depending on the environment and the amount of stress involved. When I was in the military, obsessive-compulsion was a superpower for preparing for inspections and following detailed protocols. However, it's incredibly difficult to relax and not carry the same behavior home. I have a routine for everything that is driven by a preoccupation with efficiency and optimization.

In turn, bartending can get as extreme as fine dining in terms of execution standards, so when I left working in fine dining I knew I wanted something that was a fraction of the stress. I needed to find a way to stop obsessing over every detail and lower my standards. After all, glasses didn't need to be polished to look like they've never been used and a few drops of overpour could always be fixed with a bar napkin rather than listening to a diatribe from a manager. It's much easier to think you'll simply be able to lower your expectations rather than letting go of the compulsion to maintain order in your surroundings.

Alcoholism

When you're surrounded by an ocean of alcohol behind the bar it's hard not to dive in. I come from a family of drinkers on both sides. I believe that alcoholism is on a spectrum and that bartenders are on the higher functioning end of people who drink on a daily basis. It's been a big part of my family's culture and the way we identify with being free to do what we like as Americans. After all, we have a right to make our own choices, and we shouldn't judge anyone's struggles with addiction regardless of scale. For many, it's an impulse that they're genetically driven to act on, but for those like myself it's an active choice I make to appreciate all the hard work that goes into a beverage and the way it makes me feel. I don't need it on a daily basis, but I certainly prefer it.

Alcoholism becomes a dependency issue to me when you can't function without it. Mornings with shakes from withdrawal and routinely blacking out because you can't stop; these are acts with rare exceptions that don't describe me, but I know that I've lived close to the edge for a long time. It's something that ultimately destroyed my marriage: an inability to live with each other without enabling the other person's drinking.

○ ○ ○

I was generally a teetotaler until my senior year in high school when my father started letting me have a beer or two when we visited different places and had dinner. My dad kept a small amount of beer at our apartment, but I don't recall him having a drink on a daily basis. In my recollection, my grandfather only drank on holidays like Thanksgiving; however, the rest of my family basically glorified opportunities to drink. I didn't really start to partake until I went to college and the experience was one of the only things we could do to escape. Whenever we got free for a night or two we'd usually share a large room at a hotel and have a party—usually drinking until we passed out.

Once I graduated from college, the situation grew worse for several factors: First, I was truly on my own for the first time and testing my limits; second, I was separated from my partner and going through a long period of depression; third, the culture of the military encouraged soldiers to both work and play hard; and fourth, the responsibility of leading other soldiers despite only being in my early 20s carried a significant amount of stress. In turn, I started drinking hard alcohol on a regular basis to cope and began to struggle with dependence for the first time.

My wake up call came in the form of a car crash after I drunkenly nodded off while driving on a Texas highway after midnight. The vehicle spun out of control as I jerked awake and a wire barrier in the median carved through the drivers side of my vehicle like a lightsaber, but my life was thankfully spared. The crash was so loud that people from a nearby shopping center heard the accident and crossed the highway to help me. The police arrived shortly after, and I'm convinced they let me take a cab back to the military base instead of throwing me in jail for driving under the influence due to my service. Their gracious decision spared ruining my career and shook me awake from the spell alcoholism was casting on me.

Following the incident, my drinking dramatically reduced and I started to draw healthier boundaries for myself. However, over a decade later when I started working in hospitality, my old habits began to return. Samples turned into full pours that turned into doubles that turned into entire bottles. Going to bars became more attractive than going home, and I was clearly driving toward another situation that threatened my life if I couldn't find a way to change.

Insomnia

It takes me a long time for me to get to sleep after a shift. It's hard to turn off the echo chamber in my mind replaying the day's events and projecting anxieties about the future. Ways you've been disrespected boil to the surface while the enduring worries of job sustainability, making a livable wage, and securing safe housing churn in your subconscious. You try talking it out to process, but only end up thinking about it more. You try meditating to tune out the distractions, but your senses begin detecting everything in the room. You try watching television to calm you down, but find it impossible to concentrate. In the end, we all eventually turn to self-prescribed substances as a shortcut.

○ ○ ○

Struggling to go to sleep started early in my teens with puberty. Something chemically seemed to change in me that I couldn't understand. Why was it suddenly taking so long, sometimes hours, to go to bed? It felt like I forgot a magic trick that I've been trying my entire adult life to remember. I began playing music at low volume to help cancel out the noise in my head, but the patterns in the songs grew distracting. I turned to taking hot baths to try and calm down, but I worried that the noise was too loud, so only did so on nights when it felt like I would never get to sleep. The only method that seemed to help was physical and mental exhaustion, but as an overactive teenager that didn't begin to seek out help until later in life.

It certainly didn't help that I kept how I was struggling to sleep to myself. I just figured it's something that everyone eventually figures out. Moreover, having to wake up with my father for the start of the military work day before dawn to go to day-care as a child and later to catch the 45-minute bus ride to high school in Germany only added to the problem. I've never been a morning person, but it took until I started bartending to find a schedule that worked best for me: wear myself out by staying up until after midnight and then sleep in until I'd wake up without the harshness of an alarm.

Depression

Bartending is a nomadic profession that most of us fall into when left without options that pay more than minimum wage. Being a part of a staff can provide an opportunity to commiserate about customers and complain about the ownership, but when it's just you behind the bar after midnight on a closing shift with no one to have a conversation with you start to question what the hell you're doing with your life. What future is there beyond moving into management for a few extra dollars and way more responsibility? Sure, you can always quit and find another gig (which I've done), but it's only going to be more of the same with a different decor. It's a depressing cycle that's hard to break. You end up turning to alcohol or other depressants to cope with your emotions, but they only make you feel worse.

While I was bartending, it was common for me to get home at 2am, open a bottle of wine, and start to watch television or a movie until I'd either finished the bottle or passed out from exhaustion. I had little to come home to and even less hope on the horizon. The future I'd worked so hard to achieve felt like a distant memory and the way forward was fogged by feelings of doubt and the shame of my failures.

o o o

When I was young, I can recall my mother frequently telling me to "stop feeling sorry for myself" when I got down about something and would burrow my way under the bed frame to lick my emotional wounds like an animal. I didn't really understand what she meant until much later in life, and

I still struggle with the notion that I can simply stop feeling the way I do. It's like being told to "Relax!" People often say things like "choose happiness," but those who suffer from depression know it's far more than a choice–it's a battle.

From the time I started puberty, I began to retreat more from socializing in groups. I wasn't anti-social, but I was firmly introverted and far from popular. I spent a lot of time by myself reading and doing homework or playing video games with a handful of close friends–kids I grew close to in a quick period of time, but knew I'd eventually have to leave.

Beyond reading on my own, I watched a lot of classic and critically acclaimed movies that were far too serious for a budding teenager with little concept of mature themes like marital struggles, mental illness, social injustice, and the atrocities of war. However, I was drawn to the intensity of the emotion captured in great cinema. Around the time I was 14, I decided to watch every film ever nominated for Best Screenplay that was available at the library over the summer and I still remember how concerned the librarian was that my mother was allowing me to watch such dramas.

I also listened to a lot of depressing music that for some reason beyond my understanding resonated with me as an adolescent. Imagine an acne-riddled teenager sitting on a bus listening to a Walkman playing Lilith Fair acts like Natalie Merchant and memorizing the maudlin lyrics. That's the way I went to school every day. At the time, my favorite album was actually called *Mellon Collie and the Infinite*

Sadness–122 minutes of emo-rock that served as the soundtrack of my high school years.

By the time I graduated from college, I was well prepared for living alone. While I know for many people the sound of a quiet home and absence of others can lead to loneliness, being on my own is a source of strength, so as a bartender my favorite shifts were by myself when I could keep the place clean and organized to my standards. There's a sense of relief I get from knowing I won't have to compromise for another person. When the customers leave after the last call it's equal parts liberating and boring. You get to crank up the music and listen to your favorite songs like the bar is your own. It's an opportunity to contemplate what led you to mopping the floor at 1am. There's a temptation to feel sorry for the situation you're in, like viewing the glass as half empty, but it begins to fade as you realize the power of spending time on your own to regain your strength. You reach a point when you stop obsessing about where you've been, realize that no one can change the situation you're in except yourself, and start seeing the opportunity to recover as a glass that's half full.

CHAPTER 4
THE GLASS IS HALF FULL

Starting to take medication for my mental health helped save my life. Counseling never yielded significant results in improving my mood or behavior, so when I reached the highest point of my anxiety and the lowest point of my depression while working in hospitality, I finally began to consider what life might be like if a prescription beyond self-medicating with alcohol could provide some level relief for the intensity of my feelings of hopelessness.

The moment that convinced me to begin seeking therapy was having an emotional breakdown after seeing a film called *Tully*. It's a lesser known movie featuring Charlize Theron who plays a mother trying to manage her depression while growing increasingly overwhelmed by the birth of an unexpected child at mid-life. She stops taking her medication and her grip on reality slowly spirals out of control shortly thereafter, only this fact isn't revealed to the audience until the film's finale.

Throughout the story, Tully has recurring dreams of being stuck underwater that symbolize feeling trapped. The fear of drowning is a nightmare I've struggled with since childhood. The imagery always returns whenever I'm overwhelmed by stress. Making it to the surface seems impossible. It feels like being weighted to the bottom of a lake–or a pool in my case–fighting for your life.

The film's ending was so resonant that it prompted me to write a letter to my mother. I've always had a hard time calling people and finding the right words, so I needed to spend some time thinking about exactly what I was asking. My intent wasn't to imply that my upbringing had somehow scarred me; it was a question of wanting to know more about our genetics and what I had potentially inherited.

It turned out to be a conversation that my mother had been waiting to have for a long time. I've heard that everyone knows what's wrong with you except you, and that was certainly the case with my levels of anxiety and depression. The first time I can recall the term *chemical* being used when I was growing up was a description of one of my uncles as having a "chemical imbalance" that they took medication to help regulate. As a young boy, I had no idea what this meant. Memories of visiting my mother's relatives in Michigan over the summers are some of the happiest of my childhood because family members care about me in a way that short-term friends can never substitute. I always loved the time–albeit short–that I got to spend in the rural area I was born in, so I never gave a thought to how someone in my family might feel or behave when I wasn't around. For example, it would take me decades to realize that my uncle had been diagnosed with bipolar depression.

Having a mental disorder or disability was never discussed in our household in the military community. Soldiers were conveniently considered stable enough to kill other people as long as it was on behalf of our country. When I joined the Air Force, I had to take a series of counseling sessions when I was a cadet for insubordination (compulsively speaking my mind), but was never diagnosed with any of the issues that I later realized had affected me since puberty. My college experience only made things worse by being stressed physically, mentally, and emotionally to extremes. The days would start with intense physical training before sunrise followed by long hours in challenging engineering courses and invariably end with someone telling me I should give up. Were it not for a close group of friends who helped me survive my undergraduate program, I would've listened to the hazing.

Nearly 20 years later, the feelings that haunted me from the experience caught back up to me at mid-life; except this time I finally made the decision to seek the help of a professional. I took the insurance card out of my wallet, called the number, and asked if there was a psychiatrist I could start seeing. To my shock, there were no available appointments for three months—that's how bad the mental health crisis is in our society. I was growing desperate waiting for an appointment, so I decided to see if an emergency mental health facility, primarily used for dispensing methadone, could help refer me to a psychiatrist who might not have such a long waiting list.

When I arrived the waiting room was packed with people in crisis shouting at the staff, talking on speakerphone calls, and milling about because there weren't enough chairs. A daunting security worker turned away numerous people for being on drugs while we all waited for help. The woman at the check-in desk handed me the intake form featured in the prologue of this book. My answer to nearly every question was "Yes" and I knew at that moment that this was the first step in a long road to recovery.

After over two hours of waiting, I was seated in an office with two seats across from a desk stacked with folders. A nurse practitioner entered and began speaking with me about my answers to the intake form. On the item I left blank, she asked me, "Do you have a plan?" I responded that I really didn't know anymore where I wanted to be in five years, and that's when I realized the form was actually asking whether I had started planning my suicide. I could only nod my head in the affirmative as I looked away and began to cry.

As a practitioner, she explained that she was unable to prescribe anything to me; however, she gave me the blessing of a referral to a place that could see me the following week. In the meantime, she simply recommended I go across the street to a popular health food grocery store and buy some passion flower essence in a bedside diffuser to help me sleep. My eyebrows reached a new height, but I thanked her earnestly and wished her well. I was due at the restaurant where I knew the sort of work that was awaiting, but it gave me strength realizing how hard it must be to hear stories like mine numerous times on a daily basis at their clinic. There are always people who have it harder than you; even at your lowest.

The following week, I entered another waiting room—this one void of patients and decorated with abstract paintings on the wall. Shortly after I arrived, a slender woman maybe ten years older than me with curly blonde hair motioned me toward her office. She essentially asked me the same series of questions that the clinic had, but as a psychiatrist she took a more scientific approach than holistic shopping for fruit-flavored remedies. After hearing what I had to say and judging by how on edge I was, she wrote me a prescription for a drug called Sertraline (more commonly referred to as Zoloft) that's designed to treat a combination of conditions such as depression, anxiety, post-traumatic stress, and obsessive-compulsive disorder. I thanked her for her evaluation and agreed to meet again the following week to see if the medication made any difference.

I picked up the prescription on the way to work, parked behind the restaurant, and held the bottle in my hand to consider if I really wanted to start turning to pills to solve my problems. I was more than ready emotionally but was terrified of what might happen during service if I had an adverse reaction or there were side effects. Additionally, I hadn't discussed the decision with my husband, who held the belief that taking medication only leads to dependence, so I decided to wait until my day off to speak with him.

That Sunday morning, I shared that I had seen a psychiatrist and they'd given me the option to start taking Sertraline. His response, as the son of a pastor, was that we should go to church to pray on the decision, so I obliged rather than starting an argument. After the service, he pleaded for me not to start taking medication that I might have to take for the rest of my life. With tears streaming down my face, I replied that without some sort of medical intervention I'd be meeting God–if such a consciousness exists–in the near future.

When we returned home, I drew a small blue pill from the bottle and started on a new path that I hoped would lead me toward a better place. A few hours later, I began to feel a mild nausea and it seemed like things around me were starting to feel hazy. A level of fatigue set in and I recall barely eating dinner before laying down early in bed. I didn't feel like myself and my husband, as he was quick to remind me of his warning, could tell. The effect was a far cry from a quick fix. If this was the answer I was looking for, then it was going to take time to adjust.

The following day, I took the medication again and the nausea didn't come on as strong, but the hazy effect remained. It felt like I needed glasses to focus on my surroundings–almost like I was drunk. There was no way I was going to be able to work under this new influence, so an anxiety set in that the solution I'd invested so much hope in was a failure. Despite the psychiatrist warning that it might take weeks for the effects to calm down and balance, I stopped taking the prescription after two doses. Fine dining was my only source of employment at the time, and I couldn't risk losing my job, so I sacrificed my mental health.

On my next psychiatrist visit, she took note of the symptoms and reassured me that we'd be able to find a better option that wouldn't have the same side effects. In turn, Sertraline was replaced with a combination of Lamotrigine in the morning and Quetiapine at night; medications used to manage anxiety and bipolar depression. Still weary of not being able to function at work, I waited again until Sunday before testing the medication. The shape of the blue pill was different this time, and in some small way it gave me hope to keep trying.

That day, I didn't notice much change in the afternoon, but when I took the medication in the evening I fell into a deep slumber that felt like a weighted blanket was covering me. It was probably the best sleep I'd had in months. I woke up a bit groggy, but seeing that the clock read that it was after 11am jolted me awake. I needed the rest, but if the effect lasted that long every day, then I'd have trouble getting to work on time; and that wasn't an option–at least in my mind. I flopped out of bed and began to get ready for the day; again taking the little blue pill.

That afternoon, I had to make a trip to a famous wholesale store–something I generally try to avoid because of the chaos of carts careening around like a drag race. I needed a new laptop. Something cheap and reliable was all I was looking for, but no one was in the area to help answer questions, so I walked around until I could find someone to help. Zero anxiety. The person I found to help couldn't actually help, so they left to find someone else. No problem. The manager checked the inventory and the laptop I wanted was out of stock. Do they have it at another location? Unfortunately not. May I purchase the floor model? No, sorry. Is there anything else you can try? Well, I'll tell you what, since you've been so *patient* (words I can't recall anyone ever saying about me) I'll charge you the same price, but give you the better model with more storage. Really?! I looked around me to see if there was some sort of prank being pulled. This type of good fortune has been largely elusive in my life. Was this the way people without anxiety had been living their lives–blissfully roaming the aisles of wholesale stores foraging for discounts? My mind suddenly opened to the idea that maybe I could join their ranks with the right help.

That evening, I took my prescription and fell into a deep sleep void of the nightmares of drowning. Like Tully, I began to accept the idea that medication might be able to help me see the future more clearly and allow me to stop dwelling on my past and the struggles I was facing. When I awoke, I poured a glass of water to take the second part of my medication and as I looked down into the glass it started to appear like it was half full.

STAGE 3
PREPARATION

During the preparation stage, a person might: Plan the kind of change to be made; determine how to make the change; obtain necessary resources; get rid of triggers; and put a support system in place. Individuals in this stage are building a sense of urgency regarding their desire for change.

There may be many other preparations that need to be made in your specific circumstance, such as finding a clean, safe place to start your new life. If you need help from a counselor or social worker, this is the time to get it. They may also be able to help you with other preparations. Once the necessary preparations have been made, a person is typically ready to move onto the action stage.

CHAPTER 5

A ONE-BEDROOM
OF ONE'S OWN

Moving out always brings back memories of moving in. Growing up as a military dependent we moved roughly every three years, so there are a lot of memories. I started school in Japan, moved to Michigan, Texas, California, back to Texas, and then graduated from high school in Germany. Seven schools in total with each new journey beginning by saying farewell to the last. It wasn't until I completed my military service and moved to Phoenix nearly 20 years ago that I found any sense of establishing a long-term home.

The allure of Arizona's sunshine and palm trees was a setting I quickly grew to love in contrast to the blizzards and pines of where I went to college in Colorado. Speech and Debate tournaments were often hosted at Arizona State University, so I was fortunate enough to visit the campus a number of times as a competitor when the citrus and cacti were blossoming. The independence and passion of the students in Tempe combined with the amenities of a vast city built on a convenient grid all appealed to me. I knew that when I left the Air Force I would go to graduate school, so there was never really a thought that I wouldn't go to ASU. Of all the places I've ever lived or visited, there's nothing like the desert landscape of the Southwest with its iconic red rock formations and sherbert-colored sunsets I grew up watching in westerns.

Arizona is also where I fell in love with my husband. We lived separately while I was in the military due to the bigoted "Don't Ask, Don't Tell" policy that existed at the time, so our relationship was strained by secrecy and long-distance for several years. We made our relationship work by traveling to see each other regularly. One of the happiest moments of our lives was when I separated from the military and the moving truck arrived outside our home in Phoenix. It finally felt like I had found a place to settle down.

Everything I owned fit in the spare room, so the process didn't take long. However, it quickly became clear that I was moving into someone else's meticulously curated home with little room to express my own style. Over time, the feeling grew into deep-seated resentment as my husband maintained their own offices at home as well as work while my own teaching load and graduate studies were relegated to being completed on a laptop while seated at the kitchen counter. The concept of having my own office was never even considered until the final year of my doctoral studies when I reached a breaking point. After a particularly hurtful argument I decided it was necessary to live apart until my husband finally acquiesced to adding a second desk in the spare room—a space that he insisted on referring to as the "media room" as a means of denying me any form of my own professional identity.

After six long years of graduate school earning a paltry teacher's income, a unique opportunity presented itself when I graduated to accept a role as an Associate Professor for the University of Maryland's Global Campus stationed on military installations in Europe. Combined with the power dynamics of essentially living in my husband's home as a tenant, the subconscious pattern of moving every few years had made me grow restless for the next adventure.

As it happened, the offer came on the same day that I successfully defended my doctoral dissertation and finally signaled a chance to take on a role as a breadwinner as well as have my husband experience living abroad. It was a decision that came with great trepidation, but ultimately turned out to be one of the best periods in our marriage because I finally felt like I was treated as an equal in our relationship.

While teaching in Europe I was assigned to Germany, Spain, and England over the course of nearly two years. My husband took a sabbatical to join me and enjoyed a period of revitalized productivity late in his career, publishing a textbook as well as authoring an award-winning journal article. For the first time in our marriage I felt like we'd found an equitable balance. Everything was going well until the end of his sabbatical coincided with a number of medical issues that arose (including needing a liver transplant) that necessitated our return to Arizona. It was one of the most difficult choices I've ever had to make: stay abroad thriving in a dream job or throw it all away to tend to my husband's health and comfort. I chose the latter without hesitation or regret, but it's a decision my mind has not ceased thinking about even years later.

Returning to Phoenix provided the medical attention my husband required, including eventual liver and kidney transplants, but the decision completely derailed my career and planted the seeds of resentment that would eventually grow into the root causes of our separation. My husband returned to his full-time professorship teaching two upper-level courses while I was forced to return to an entry-level role teaching six large-scale introductory courses in Flagstaff at Northern Arizona University (two hours away from our home) to make ends meet.

I was working twice as hard for half as much income and the situation quickly grew untenable–particularly once my husband decided to retire without my consent. Prioritizing his preferences came at the sacrifice of my own needs. From my perspective, he needed to continue to work until I could find a similar role to what I had lost in Europe, but he wasn't willing to wait for what we both knew was unlikely to ever happen again.

Left with figuring out how to sustain our lifestyle on a teacher's pension and my meager salary, I started working at a restaurant that would completely change my life. For those who haven't read my previous memoir, *A Year in Waiting*, I can tell you that it recounts a period that essentially served as my mid-life crisis. I reached a point in my life where I felt trapped and hopeless. Pleas for help seemed to fall on deaf ears and applying for jobs on a daily basis was met with painfully routine rejections. I could no longer see a future for myself. Anxiety led to insomnia and depression led to isolation.

I started bartending to make ends meet and the hours required my absence at home. I couldn't remember the last time I'd truly been happy instead of smiling in photos to project an image of prosperity. Talk therapy proved to be a dead-end and taking medication became a source of contention. In turn, arguing became a love language for desperately trying to find solutions, but the problems had grown too overwhelming. The only two options that seemed viable at the time were suicide or leaving; so I made the most difficult decision of my life and chose to try to find a way out of the situation on my own.

Staying with friends was only feasible for a few days and moving in with family was something my pride wouldn't allow me to consider. It was early March of 2020 and COVID loomed more ominously every day. I needed shelter, but my options on a part-time teacher and bartender's wages were considerably limited. Enter The Capri: a sprawling collection of massive four-story mid-century block construction apartments that formerly served as a singles development in the swinging 60s that gradually devolved into Section 8 housing in the heart of Phoenix by the time I became a tenant. The location was a mile away from the bar where I worked, the price was within my budget, and there was a scarcity of seven TOTAL apartments available within a five mile radius at the time, so I snapped up the only unit they had sight unseen and moved in the following week.

When I initially moved to The Capri I optimistically tried to be neighborly and say hello to people, but the onset of the pandemic led to paranoia of being around others since adopting masks was viewed as an extreme safety measure that wasn't necessary in public. Elevator rides became places of confrontation, and the public amenities were gradually closed off, so I never made any friends in the complex. Many of the residents would sit on their patios on their phones while perpetually smoking for what seemed like the entirety of the day—a practice that continued long after the pandemic—so I couldn't identify with being so stagnant.

As one might expect, it didn't take long to realize the many negative attributes of living at The Capri: a perpetual haze of marijuana smoke that lingered like a fog; daily appearances by cop cars, fire trucks, or emergency services; nightly screams ranging from terror to ecstasy; weekly fire alarms that could raise the dead; and public spaces in a ceaseless state of disrepair due to acts such as urinating in the often-broken elevator and pranks like leaving crayons in the dryer. As a result, climbing four flights of stairs became routine and I ended up having to wash my clothes at a coin laundry (or my Aunt's house in a pinch) like a college student for three years. However, all of this paled in comparison to being stuck with radiant coils for heating and cooling instead of air conditioning—an essential part of surviving the infamous summer heat in Phoenix. I began to feel like I moved from one cage to a considerably hotter one, but the isolation was exactly what I needed to recover: a place of my own. From the vantage point of the apartment's patio, I could see a sliver of the top of Camelback Mountain peering over the edge of the neighboring building, so I tried to focus on the positive view in the distance.

CHAPTER 6
SELF-CARE

Reducing my anxiety and curbing my depression provided a newfound mental composure that allowed me to reevaluate my emotional state. Alone in my one-bedroom apartment during COVID quarantine, I finally admitted that I'd fallen into a number of self-destructive patterns going to great lengths to take care of others and finally began to acknowledge that it was time to start making healthier decisions for myself. Chief among these realizations was to stop deferring to the wants of others and start considering my own needs instead of suppressing my emotions. It was time to own that no one else could act on my behalf, so I set about asking myself a series of questions from the perspective of a neutral observer. Essentially, I wanted to understand–for better or worse–*why* I've made certain choices that characterize my identity, evaluate whether to continue or change, and seek out practices that might be able to provide some degree of therapy. Within popular culture, the practice is often referred to as *self-care*.

Coloring

I moved into The Capri with a suitcase of clothes, blow-up mattress, and laptop. White walls and a hollow space. My apartment stared at me like a blank sheet of paper. I was starting a new chapter in my life, and this time I wanted to be the one holding the pen. It may sound silly, but I was done with the color purple. Not the movie, but the actual color–my ex-husband's favorite and a signal of possession. The home we'd built had reached a suffocating level of purple: kitchen towels, plates, glasses, cooking utensils, blankets, vases, placemats, shower curtains, every type of clothing, paintings, and the list goes on like 50 shades of lilac, plum, mauve, violet, and amethyst. By the time I decided to leave, the only thing about the color I could still tolerate was listening to the song *Purple Rain*.

The following week, our lawyers agreed to allow me to collect my personal items that weren't considered community property, so I rented the smallest U-Haul truck available to pick up my few belongings: a couch, chair, makeshift desk, computer, the rest of my clothes, and a few boxes of mementos and books. As I turned onto our street, my former husband drove by in the opposite direction, and our eyes met at the intersection. It was the last time I saw him.

To my surprise, two of his best friends–a pastor and a business partner, both female–were waiting for me inside to "make sure I didn't steal anything." Steal. From my own home. As my eyes scanned the living room, I quickly realized that nearly all of the items had purple sticky notes placed on them. Yes, even the sticky notes were purple. Items that were claimed to stay in place as *his*. I rolled my eyes, told them I had no need for anything purple, and made my way to our spare bedroom where nearly all of my possessions were collected like they were being donated to Goodwill. With the help of a friend from the restaurant where I used to work, we loaded the couch, chair, and TV stand (without a television since they caught me trying to take something with a purple sticker) into the half-filled U-Haul.

As the last box was loaded and I pulled down the metal roller, the pastor and partner approached me with arms outstretched for hugs. I turned my back to them in response—my body language screaming "No you don't!" "We'll pray for you," said the pastor; and "We love you," said the partner. But I never heard from or saw them again.

I firmly agree that actions speak louder than words, and I was through with being surrounded by *friends* who never took action when I asked for help from the church or intervened when I finally admitted to his family and co-workers how bad his drinking had become. Our relationship had choked me to the point of turning purple.

○ ○ ○

When I finally felt like I could breathe again, I took account of my surroundings. White walls, black counters, silver appliances, weathered vinyl flooring, and far too many mirrors. It was time to make this place my own. So what did I do? I went to the store and started buying everything I needed in my favorite color: teal. Lamp shades, shower curtains, candles, kitchen utensils, tupperware, bath robe, potted plants, dish towels, and my bedspread—a return to the type I'd had when I was in grade school. I surrounded myself with items I could claim as my own in an attempt to find a sense of emotional security moving forward.

Why teal? It's unclear to me how anyone chooses their favorite color, but faced with selecting one my intuition always gravitates toward shades of green and blue. In the humanities, these often symbolize tranquility and the natural world as well as loyalty and affluence, so it's possibly a matter of being drawn to such values. Perhaps that's why I'm drawn to the way turquoise and mid-century aquamarine hues contrast with the rust colors that characterize the landscape of the Southwest. The femininity of pink, passion of red, energy of orange, and happiness of yellow have never suited me; nor have the binaries associated with black and white. I'm someone who's gray in the spectrum.

Given more introspection, the memory occurred to me while writing this passage that the wedding colors of my father's marriage to my step-mother were teal and purple; the same as my own. I'm not sure whom the compliment came from, but I was told at the wedding that teal matched the color of my eyes–the same as my father's–so I guess it stuck in my subconscious that I wanted to be just like him. My father and I both fell in and out of love with the same regal and prideful type of person that purple represents. In moving forward, I knew that I finally needed to embrace my own true colors.

Gardening

My last errand before the onset of quarantine was to stop by a big box homeware store. Not for lumber or screws, but for plants. Everyone looked at me like I was crazy walking through the crowded aisles with my gloves, mask, and sunglasses on for protection. I bypassed the long lines of people hoarding items like paper goods and water figuring that my utilities would still be available. However, the thought occurred to me that plants might be in short supply, so it helped at least feel more sustainable on my own. In some small way it also gave me the responsibility of tending for something that needed my help in order to grow.

When you take care of plants, they take care of you. Sustenance, flavor, medicine. The same goes for the people around you. You reap what you sow. There was so little in my life when I desperately started bartending that it felt like the earth had been salted. It forced me to uproot my life and plant new seeds—to cultivate my surroundings and nurture them the best I could so they could do the same for me.

As I settled into my new space, I filled six planter boxes on my patio with herbs, peppers, and tomatoes. Perhaps it was also a homage to my grandfather who worked for the Department of Agriculture in Michigan and had always maintained an edible garden. It harkened back to the times of victory provisions during the war—contributing on a personal scale in order to help aid the fight for a better future. A way of providing when there was little to gather and planting crops for future generations.

○ ○ ○

When I transitioned from fine dining into bartending, I wouldn't say my skill set grew, but my body and emotions were finally able to be attended to in the way they had long been neglected. It came as a small irony that there was a lonely succulent near our entrance that I became responsible for watering. When I arrived it was wilting like myself, but given some time it began to thrive. Once I settled into the rhythms of the day at the bar—slow opening, busy happy hour, late night regulars, and a quiet closing—I started nurturing the space itself while watering the patrons.

Once business dried up at the start of the pandemic, there was a day that I received a dollar tip and it was a particularly low moment for me financially as well as feeling emotionally worthless for the first time. When I shared the moment on social media, a friend sent me a small bank transfer with the suggestion that I buy something that I wouldn't normally purchase. As it happened, I needed to pick up some fertilizer that afternoon, so I returned to the homeware store. While I was waiting in line, I spotted a beautiful red and green variegated cactus blooming. *Why not buy it with the unexpected gift?* Unsure of the name of the cactus, I looked at the label and it made me genuinely smile for the first time in weeks: Luck Plant. I immediately knew it had found the right home.

Gaming

One of the happiest moments of my childhood was when my father shocked me with the first Nintendo gaming system for Christmas when I was six years old. I can still remember unwrapping the shiny red paper and being overwhelmed with excitement. The console came with three games: *Super Mario Bros*, *Duck Hunt*, and *Track & Field*. I'd played the original Atari games when visiting my cousins, but this was a whole new level of interaction. Instead of staying on the same fixed screen, Mario scrolled to the right as you progressed through the different stages of the game; *Duck*

Hunt called for the use of an orange and gray plastic gun that tracked wherever you pointed on the screen; and *Track & Field* came with a sort of plastic *Twister*-style mat with large circles called a "power pad" that captured the movement of your feet. I marveled at how my father beat them all, and so I set out to do the same. With practice, gaming improved my coordination and understanding of strategy as a means for overcoming challenges.

Gaming also offers an escape. As an only child with a single parent who worked long hours, I found myself more and more immersed in video games for the interaction they offered beyond more passive forms of entertainment like books and watching VHS tapes. Yes, like anything entertaining, video games can be a potential distraction, but they can also show us ways to solve problems in our actual lives. Challenges you're stuck on for days, maybe even months or years trying to conquer, you eventually figure out a way to move past (or sometimes side-step with a cheat code). It's a lesson that's served me well throughout my education. During the most productive periods of my life, I've always played video games.

Over the years, gaming technology has steadily improved to feature more visually stunning graphics and immersive stories. There are many different genres, but my favorites have always been puzzle-based games where you have to use problem solving to advance through trials. My favorite game has always been the different versions of *The*

Legend of Zelda. Essentially, you're sent on a quest to save a damsel in distress from forces of evil and must collect an array of different weapons and resources to overcome increasingly more difficult enemies. It's the archetype for the design of hundreds of derivative games that would follow and mirror the sort of incremental improvement that you go through as you advance through life. We're all on quests.

○ ○ ○

People in bars are almost always playing a game of some sort trying to meet new friends or find partners. Guests come to bars to socialize and get out of their homes to engage with others. Video games are no different, but there's a contrast between interpersonal skills and online interaction. The two are different, and I can attest that interpersonal skills are waning; especially as someone who's taught communication courses for over a decade. People can do more complicated tasks using cutting-edge digital tools, but they often struggle to work collaboratively. It's like the dreaded group project that always gets accomplished by a single student at the last minute. Not everyone is capable of winning a game by themselves. Most people need help, and maybe that's where bartenders like myself come in to assist as facilitators–or maybe it's the booze.

Before people meet for a date if they've been matched on an app, they already know far more about each other–at least on a surface level–than previous generations would know. It's constant access to information and being emboldened by communicating through a device that alters how people interact in person. Today, there's way more emphasis on hooking up or hanging out as part of a group of friends rather than the intimidating concept of meeting face to face. It's a different type of game.

One of the bars I worked at actually had gaming systems installed with a series of televisions for people to break the ice. In the quiet hours when I opened or closed the bar, I'd take a break to play on the old systems out of nostalgia, but also competition. It reached a point where we started putting hi-scores on the chalkboard and nearly all of the records belonged to me.

Moreover, hosting trivia nights was a way of linking my career in teaching to my time behind the bar. In a small way, it helped guests get to know me better and provided them a reason to come in for something fun to do. We'd partner with local distributors and have them sponsor trivia nights. It was always fun, and one of the events I took pride in hosting on those evenings.

In a way, I think it helped distract me from how depressing tending bar had become as the guests–and in turn tips–had fallen off significantly. Looking at the numbers as I closed every day, I couldn't see how the place was making money. Things were perpetually broken, our beverage list had been decimated, and our taps had grown stale. Management had become MIA, and the ownership wasn't putting anything into the business or promotions, so it was clear we were no longer sustainable. In turn, it was only a matter of time before we closed like so many establishments during the pandemic.

All the bartenders knew what was eventually coming, but one day I received a text stating that the bar would be closing for good within a week. A text. There was virtually no opportunity to apply for jobs elsewhere, so I began to panic, yet again. The bar owners seemed like they were playing games with the staff, and we had clearly lost despite our best efforts to keep the place open. Hi-scores didn't matter. It was Game Over.

○ ○ ○

When I got married, I packed my gaming systems into a box where they stayed unused for nearly 15 years. After we separated, left on my own like in my childhood, I unpacked the box and plugged my PlayStation in as an escape during the pandemic. It was a way to immerse myself in settings like roaming the wild west on horseback, battling gods from Greek mythology, and rebelling against the Empire in far away galaxies.

Today, video games exist as immersive virtual worlds. You're no longer just interacting with the game, but you're collaborating/competing with other players from across the globe. At first glance, it's easy to rush to judgment that engaging with video games is a "waste of time," but I can attest that if you limit your screen time and play games that engage your problem solving skills they can be used to activate your thinking and serve as a warmup for the work you need to accomplish. As someone who's applied for hundreds of jobs, I can attest that landing a position is like beating a particularly difficult game. For a long period of time I tried to figure out how to overcome the challenge by myself, but I eventually realized that if I collaborated with my friends then the chances of winning significantly increased.

The moment came when I reconnected with one of my former professors through social media. *Stranger Things* was a popular television show at the time, and we enjoyed talking about the nostalgia for the 80s that it featured–particularly the game *Dungeons and Dragons*. The original was a sort of board game that I had never played, but always wanted to learn. It's essentially an exercise in shared imagination where you're part of a band of adventurers sent on varying quests where dice are rolled as a form of randomization so you never know exactly how interactions will turn out.

Watching the characters on *Stranger Things* playing reminded me that I'd always wanted to figure out what the game was all about, but I'd never known anyone who knew something about it until the subject came up in conversation. It turned out my former professor played online via Zoom on a bi-weekly basis with a group of friends and family members around Salt Lake City. I asked if they'd let me sit in on a session, and they welcomed me with open arms. By the next meeting, I'd created a character who was a portly bard capable of inflicting psychic damage with songs and verbal jabs. As the campaign advanced, *Dungeons and Dragons* turned into a sort of support group for the majority of us who struggle with social anxiety. I was largely alone during this time period, but crafting the narrative every other week turned into a project that helped me feel less alone.

Games allow us to simulate what we might do in a given situation and deal with the consequences of those actions. For example, if I decide to search a tomb for treasure, I should be prepared for a ghost to appear and try to attack me. That way, when you have a difficult decision to make at work, you can put yourself in the position of simulating all the potential outcomes before you make a decision. It's good practice for staying patient and considerate instead of racing to action and making a false move that makes you have to restart.

Smiling

For the majority of my life I've avoided showing my teeth when smiling. I'm not sure why, but it probably started by copying the men in my family when I was younger and gradually grew into being too embarrassed to show my chipped and crooked teeth in high school. I had terrible acne once I reached puberty and couldn't handle the thought of orthodontics further bruising my self-esteem. I'd seen kids with braces picked on and complain about how painful they were, so I wanted nothing of that. My acne was so bad I actually skipped school pictures by going to the bathroom when given a hall pass and then returning as if I'd been with the photographer.

Showing your teeth while smiling was something I thought was reserved for actors and people with perfectly aligned teeth like the models in magazines like the issues of *Esquire* I read through as an adolescent. Instead, I adopted a smirk that came across as smug in retrospect. Part of it was cosmetic, but the other half was never feeling very happy. I had no need to hold on to the image of myself at the time and not much to smile about anyway.

It didn't help that I developed a fear of the dentist after I chipped my front teeth playing softball. I can still recall fielding a hit at shortstop and how the ball bounced out of the glove like an uppercut smashing into my face. Blood immediately started streaming down from my mouth and I began to involuntarily sob. It was the first time I'd felt that level of pain and the procedure the dentist had to take was even worse.

Moreover, I witnessed both of my parents go through agonizing dental visits. When I was young, my mother went through a series of surgeries to align her jaw, and my father had his front teeth violently knocked out in a boxing ring that's affected him throughout his life. I can recall actually going to a place nicknamed "Molar Village" in Mexico for him to have a procedure to implant anchors of tissue for replacing the bridge in his teeth and he couldn't bite with his front teeth for nearly a year.

○ ○ ○

The first thing guests notice about a bartender is whether they greet you with a smile. For me, this was a form of emotional labor like faking an upbeat attitude. I became a bartender out of sheer knowledge and work ethic, so the way I was perceived by guests wasn't at the top of my priorities. I needed the money, but I was rarely in a mood to smile about that fact. In turn, my tips were usually lower because I didn't play the game of feigning attraction or interest in the average patron. Like Billy Bob Thornton says as a barber in *The Man Who Wasn't There*, "I just cut the hair."

It's not that I didn't kindly welcome guests, promptly attend to their needs, and ensure the space was constantly being maintained and cleaned. I have one of those resting faces that people misinterpret as discontent. Waiting tables had taken part of my soul by showing me just how unreasonable and demanding, if not altogether condescending, people can be. They expect you to be happy to serve them, and that's a problem I struggle with as someone providing a service. Bartending shouldn't be like working at McDonalds. The concept of "service with a smile" sets performative expectations. Why should someone have to act like they're excited to be in customer-facing positions? American culture is built around outward perceptions that can be exhausting to manage. There's always an assumption that people should like what they "do" professionally, and if they don't they should do something else. That's rarely an option in the service industry.

A job like bartending requires an extra layer of performing for guests from the moment they enter to the signature on their tab. People expect not only to be served, but to be entertained, and it all begins with appearance. It's a fact that attractive bartenders make more money. That's why so many young and well-groomed workers are in the profession–it's easy money as long as you look and play the part.

○ ○ ○

While I was bartending, it had been a long time since I felt like things were getting better in my life and an even longer time since I'd felt genuinely happy. One day during an argument with my ex-husband he asked "When have you ever been happy?" And my reply took an uncomfortably long silence reflecting on how bad things had become for me emotionally. "The summer we first met," I eventually replied.

That was the first time I can recall ever seeing a picture with my teeth on display. It was at a moment when I'd fallen in love for the first time.

The first thing I decided to do once my divorce was finalized was fix the things about me that I'd put off because I felt they were a selfish use of our finances and time. No longer saddled with those obligations, I finally decided to do something for myself: straighten and align my teeth as a way of bolstering my self-esteem and trying to find the confidence to smile again.

I'd avoided traditional braces out of self-image issues and felt that I didn't have the charisma of Tom Cruise getting braces at mid-life, but I discovered a new technique called lingual braces where the brackets are placed on the interior of the teeth. The process required several detailed X-rays and a panoramic view of my mouth, followed with analysis by my orthodontist to create a plan, and the connection of wires that would be attached to brackets glued behind my teeth. The process was daunting, but I decided that it would be worth it to make a significant change in my appearance to help reflect my slowly growing confidence in myself being able to live a life independent of a relationship.

The installation of the brackets and wires took hours and felt like the punishment scene in *Brazil*. Staring at the ceiling through orange-tinted glasses and my mouth clamped open the entire procedure, I couldn't stop doubting whether I was doing the right thing. Why was it suddenly so important to go through such a painful process? The answer that calmed my mind and gave me the sense of purpose over the course of having the wires and brackets gradually adjusted over the course of the next two years was the acknowledgement that I'd been growing in the wrong direction like my teeth for far too long. It was time to start reversing that process and taking steps toward finding the strength to look in the mirror and see someone smiling back.

STAGE 4
ACTION

During the action stage, people engage in the bulk of what they would consider to be recovery. They change either their behavior or their surroundings in order to enact change. By enacting the change for which they have been preparing, people going through recovery build a sense of accomplishment. Although this stage often requires the most effort on the part of the person, it's also the most important stage since it will be the bedrock for their continued recovery.

While it takes a great deal of time and effort to get to this stage, those that get here report feelings of satisfaction and self-worth that their internal efforts were valuable after all. This is often the first stage that others can see from the outside looking in.

CHAPTER 7

THE EXERCIST

Once I found a place of security and my emotions stabilized, it was time to start tending to my physical health. I'd reached a point where I was avoiding looking at myself in the mirror, unable to face myself. No one can change your self perception but you. People may try to influence the way you look and feel, but ultimately you are the one who chooses to accept or reject those influences. Honesty is key to acknowledging the areas you feel depressed about and considering how you might grow away from the patterns that led to where you are. I not only wanted to change the way I was thinking about myself, but the way I looked. My complexion had dried out from habitual drinking, my back was starting to give out from long hours of labor on my feet without breaks, and I'd lost an unhealthy amount of weight because I was making so little that I stopped buying groceries to save money. I looked and felt defeated, so I started to focus on how I could make corrective actions. I needed to start taking better care of my body, so I stopped drinking hard alcohol, paid better attention to my nutrition, and started exercising.

Since I met my ex-husband in 2004, I'd fallen into his pattern of drinking several double gin and tonics on a daily basis. Before that time, I'd grown up drinking beer in Germany in small amounts as a teenager and advanced to binge drinking on the rare weekend of leave when I was in military school. Once I graduated and was sent to my first assignment in Texas, unable to have my partner join me due to the "Don't Ask, Don't Tell" policy of the service at the time, I started drinking more heavily and by myself–signs that led to the start of a long period of depression while living alone. It didn't help that I started eating my feelings by consuming enough food for two people and quickly grew overweight for the first time in my life.

A year later, when I was assigned to Southern California, my wake up call came when I was pulled over late on a Sunday speeding home after having too much to drink. The highway patrolman pulled me over and I can still remember how the steel handcuffs braced my wrists in a vice grip as he dumped me into the back seat and hauled me to the police station for Driving Under the Influence. There are few feelings worse than the shame of being photographed and fingerprinted in the moments before you're thrown in jail to dry out. The following morning, the police released me at the break of dawn and I took a cab to where my car had been towed. Then came the profound embarrassment of informing my leadership of my misconduct–a mistake that essentially derailed my career as a military officer.

As a penalty for my misconduct, I was suspended from driving for a year, lost my qualification for any merit-based service medals, and my promotion was delayed indefinitely–not to mention the punishment from the state after pleading guilty that cost thousands of dollars. It would've been so easy to give up on my future in the days that followed being pulled over and jailed, but the repercussions actually served as an awakening and helped curb my depression by forcing me to start finding a way to feel better through exercise.

Running

As a kid with abundant energy, my parents used to play a game with me where they would try to exhaust me by having me run to different goals, say a tree in a park, and time me. When I'd return, they'd claim that I'd run to the wrong tree and have me go again. Humorously, this was a haze that I'd later encounter during Basic Training, but I've never had a problem keeping up when it comes to running. By the time I started middle school when my father was assigned to Texas, I could already run a mile in 5:18 and was immediately recruited to run the 1,500 and 3,000 meters for the track team. My favorite sports were soccer and basketball, in which I could be part of a team, but my success at athletics was always rooted in speed and endurance. What I lacked in skill, I made up for with hustle.

My maternal grandfather was also a prominent influence on my running because he had competed in all of the major national marathons numerous times. After his brother died from a massive heart attack in his 40s, he quit smoking and dedicated himself to improving his health. Running became his addiction. He'd take me out to train with him and literally run circles around me in his 60s. I marvelled at his boxes of trophies and wanted to be just like him. When I reached high school, I joined the cross-country team and performed well, but my heart wasn't in competing as an individual. I always pushed myself too hard with something to prove and would often throw up into a trash can at the end of races, so I eventually transitioned into exercising on my own instead of adding the self-imposed pressure of competition.

Beyond sports, running became a way for me to get out of my head by pushing to a point of exhaustion. By the time I became a senior and started training to go to the Air Force Academy, my daily routine would include running a three-mile path from our apartment housing across the Frankfurt airport's flight line all the way to the military base's gym to work out and then run back home. Friends of my father who recognized me would honk their horns as they drove past and I took pride in doing something so physically challenging that most people would never attempt. That's the sort of exercise it took for me to distance my mind from whatever anxieties I was experiencing and focus on the horizon. It's a practice that's always helped me stay in shape when I can stick to a pattern of regularly exercising.

Once I completed my service in the military and transitioned into teaching in higher education, I went through a period of lethargy because the culture was completely different from the activity level maintained by soldiers. Academia centered on either standing in a room speaking at length or sitting at a desk typing until your eyes would wear out. Thankfully, my best friend who lived down the street suggested that we start jogging together so he could lose some weight. It took him a few weeks to reach a mile without walking, but he kept at it and I was happy to encourage him. We started setting a routine for days of the week we would run, and gradually we were able to go a few miles on the dusty trails behind our homes that wove through the desert.

After we reached a year, we were both feeling acclimated enough to set a goal of running a half marathon together. Of all the races we could have selected, my wine-loving running partner decided we should travel to Dundee Hills in Oregon for a course that traced through the famous vineyards in the area. With little foresight, the day before the race was spent blissfully sampling the famous Pinot Noir produced in the region. There's nothing quite like starting a half marathon with a raging hang-over, but we took our time trotting up and down the hills of the vineyard walking when we needed to rest, but intent on reaching our goal. Awaiting us at the finish line were bottles of wine to celebrate, but we wanted nothing but water and Ibuprofen.

Over the course of the next few years, we kept up our routine and added a few 5K and 10K races along the way, but we held back on longer distances until we decided that our ultimate goal would be to finally run a full marathon just before my 30th birthday. This time we chose to stay close to home and try making it to the end of the Rock 'n' Roll Arizona marathon where bands are stationed at most of the mile markers to serve as motivation to keep going. I can still remember how unseasonably cold it was at the start of the race and we tried to stay warm by wearing trash bags for insulation. Shivering with the rest of the crowd as the gun sounded to start the race, our bodies eventually warmed up and we made steady progress listening to all the bands along the way. At the halfway mark we took a break to walk and considered whether we should finish. The route is entirely on closed roads, which are subtly graded to wick water away when it rains. My right foot was starting to hurt because of the angle, but we made the decision to press on.

By the time we made it to mile 20, I was having to favor my left foot to keep going, but we knew from the runner's high at that point that there was no way we weren't going to make it to the finish line—even though I'd later find that I'd fractured my foot. It's an accomplishment I'll always celebrate because we couldn't have done it without each other's motivation to persevere. I keep my bib number in a frame, and it always brings a smile to my face reflecting on my grandfather's example and how proud he'd be of us.

Swimming

My parents decided to have me learn to swim before I could walk, but swimming was something I had always done for leisure–or survival training in the military–not fitness. When I moved to England to teach, our flat in Cambridge was next door to a fitness center with a large indoor pool. It was a bitterly cold winter when I arrived, so exercising indoors was much more attractive than freezing. Fortunately, the gym had an array of free introductory classes. Looking through the options, I spotted a stroke clinic that I figured would help me learn proper technique beyond treading water. Indeed, it completely changed the way I swam because I'd never been taught correctly how to breathe, maintain body position, and alternate strokes. After improving my technique through classes, I began to follow workout schedules and found a rhythm of going nearly every morning while the gym was typically quiet. There was something calming about focusing on counting strokes, paying attention to proper technique, and the monotony of following the black line at the bottom of the lane. It was difficult at first, but as the months went by my body adapted to the challenge of the workouts and eventually grew the leanest I've ever been.

○ ○ ○

Like many Americans, I became a fan of swimming watching Michael Phelps break numerous records at the 2016 Olympics, and in an unexpected turn of events began a correspondence with his coach, Bob Bowman, through social media. He had recently accepted an offer to take the reins of the team at Arizona State University and published a book that I'd drawn some sound advice from, so I was excited by the best in the world moving to coach my alma mater. The timing coincided with the end of my husband's sabbatical and the onset of his health problems, which pressured me to leave my role in Europe and return to teach at ASU, so I looked forward to the prospect of meeting Bowman and potentially finding a way to work together.

Once I was back on campus, we got the chance to meet in person, but he wasn't interested in getting to know each other as he was on social media. We'd regularly exchanged messages in an ongoing *Words with Friends* game and I admit that I probably expected too much from someone who clearly saw me as a fan and not an analyst who could seriously contribute to the swimming team winning a National Championship. Still, I took one of the messages of his book to "always stay persistent" to achieve your goals and committed to: 1) attending all of the swim meets as a student taking notes to really learn the finer points of the sport; and 2) learning more about the physical stress and mechanics first-hand by attending clinics that the team offered.

As it happened, one of my colleagues mentioned in a conversation that her husband was a former Olympic swimmer, Bill Mettler, and that I should try going with him to daily Masters-level workouts. I arrived not knowing what to expect and certainly felt like a fish out of water among the majority of athletes with lean waists and broad shoulders who had competed in college. I was way out of my league, but Bill met my anxiety with a patient smile. He was closing in on 70 years old with a husky build and permanently tanned skin from a lifetime spent in pools. I thought my conditioning was strong at the time, but swimming quickly humbles you if you're not acclimated to the distance of workouts that generally last an hour. Bill made everything look so effortless as he glided through the water. For every two strokes I'd take, he'd only need one. This was a man, very much like my grandfather, who had committed his fitness to a lifetime sport and I quickly grew to appreciate his friendship and mentoring.

Suddenly, swimming had become a huge part of my life between workouts with Bill, cheering on students at meets, and continuing to correspond with Bob. My husband and I helped cook for the team on Thanksgiving and donated to the travel budget around the holidays. I even ended up with several athletes, including swimmers, in my spring courses. However, my enthusiasm for supporting the team was erased as quickly as it started when I lost my job after failing two football players in the inciting incident for *A Year in Waiting*.

During the aftermath of my firing from butting heads with the athletic department, an article was published on the front page of *USA Today* on Bob Bowman exposing an act of sexual harassment in which he repeatedly texted one of the female swimmers from the Olympic team trying to pursue her younger brother. Disgusted, I stopped "following" him on social media. They say to avoid meeting your heroes because you'll only be disappointed, and I learned the hard way. As my final act on campus, I took his book to the aquatics center and threw it in the pool to drown. He kept his job without punishment and I haven't set foot on campus since.

Left to deal with the fallout from ASU, and sickened by Bowman's conduct, I fell into another period of depression that led me to stop exercising at all–much less swimming. By the time I found another job and started teaching in Flagstaff at Northern Arizona University along with the added challenge of working in fine dining full time, there were no hours left for my fitness anymore. After all, I was already walking roughly five miles during a shift. It took the better part of a year until I was reminded how valuable exercising can be not only for your body, but for your mental health, too.

Yoga

I started going to hot yoga with my ex-husband because they weren't able to do most other athletic activities. Going to a gym for him was out of the question, but laying on a mat in an overheated room was like a tropical plant basking in the warmth. On my day off, we started going to yoga together on Sundays and it served as a nice way to decompress after the work week. For me, it turned into a personal challenge to learn all the movements to the best of my ability and try to focus on the present moment. Every yoga session begins in child's pose and carries through a variety of stretches and balancing exercises that ultimately ends in corpse pose–a representation of the entire life cycle in an hour.

Yoga studios take varying approaches to the practice such as cranking dance music at peak volume or exercising silence before the start of class, but the poses are virtually the same wherever you go. You listen to an instructor provide prompts and try to follow along as a group. By the time you're 15 minutes into a session you'll be drenched in sweat and unable to think about anything other than focusing on the instructor's prompts and your breathing. In through the nose; out through the mouth.

When COVID arrived, my studio started doing free online sessions that I took part in by using a mat in my bedroom and propping my phone against the wall. I kept up with my usual classes for a few weeks until the novelty wore off. Being in a room by yourself is a significantly different experience compared to a communal sense of presence. When you make it to the more challenging poses during the flow portion at the heart of the sequence it always helps to see everyone around you trying to keep up as well.

Once my yoga studio reopened, the cost grew to $30 per class and essentially priced me out of going. However, gyms were desperate to have people return after being forced to shut down for public safety. Fortunately, the gym closest to me dramatically reduced its membership enrollment fees as it reopened close to my birthday. In turn, I used the gifts I received from my family to invest in my health–something I'd avoided out of a combination of lethargy and financial trepidation. For less than the cost of going to yoga twice a week, I could go as much as I wanted. I didn't have very much money coming in, and the type of work I'd been doing was significantly tough on my body. Again, I recognized that I needed to turn things around, so I joined a gym and started to find a pattern of exercise including yoga that I rigorously followed on a daily basis.

Weight Lifting

When businesses started to re-open after the pandemic, I accepted a job working in a French-style bistro connected to a wine bar. Months into the role, I began to develop hip and back pain from returning to standing for long periods of time. Without benefits or the funds to pay for treatment, I kept going by taking handfuls of Ibuprofen and trying to reduce the inflammation with an ice pack in the morning and evening. By the time things came to a head I was barely able to get out of bed. What started as back pain expanded to my hip and eventually turned into numbness in my entire leg. An hour into a shift, I couldn't really feel my left foot, but I kept trudging on because I didn't have any other options for work.

Over Christmas, I finally reached out to my aunt, a physical therapist, and she gave me instructions on a series of exercises that provided some relief. She said that I needed physical therapy; however, I didn't know how to pay for it so I tabled the thought. Finally, one day I woke up and couldn't get out of bed. I was writhing in pain and was on the verge of calling 911. I lived across the street from an urgent care, but I was in too much pain to get out of bed, much less walk. I ended up passing out from the pain. When I awoke, I was at least able to stand, but putting clothes on was a Herculean task. It took me nearly an hour to get to a point where I could get out of my apartment and cross the street.

Unfortunately, the urgent care didn't open for another hour, so I slumped by the front door and waited for someone, anyone, to help me. Eventually, a nurse opened the front door and let me in. A few minutes later a doctor saw me and immediately prescribed painkillers—something I generally avoid because of their addictive qualities, but desperately needed at the moment.

The toll of working on your feet for long hours is tremendous compared to desk jobs where you're primarily seated. Most bartenders don't take the time to stay in shape. Instead, the solution often comes in the form of drugs and alcohol to numb the pain. Most of the bartenders I know, and to a degree myself, are high-functioning alcoholics. They've been living a difficult life for such a long time that they've been seasoned. Just try going out for drinks with a bartender or cook. You'll have a hard time keeping up.

Your body needs to be like iron to stand the stress and physical labor of hospitality work, so I started lifting weights to strengthen my core and back to counteract the pain I was suffering. When I was playing sports in school, weight lifting was a part of practice. I learned proper technique at an early age, but the downside was that I gained too much muscle while I was still growing and it led to stretch marks across my back like tiger stripes. It didn't help that I went through basic training at 18 years old and my body was still adapting. Instead of lifting weights, the military placed a heavy emphasis on calisthenics like push-ups, pull-ups, and sit-ups. It was common to do hundreds of pushups and dozens of pull-ups a day, so my strength and endurance were at their peak.

Now, over 20 years later, my body could barely lift itself up–much less someone else–so I made the decision to get back to some semblance of strength by starting to go to the weight room at my gym twice a week. I wasn't trying to get buff like the teenagers and bodybuilders taking up space on machines while checking their phones; I just wanted to stop feeling weak. I recorded my baseline for being able to do three sets of 10 for each exercise, created a circuit that worked each muscle group, and eventually added more weight every other week. Combined with physical therapy on my back and stretching in yoga, the process took approximately seven months to reach a point where my body felt bulletproof. At 5'7" and 150 lbs, I went from lifting 100 lbs to 200 lbs with my arms and 200 lbs to 400 lbs with my legs. It felt like I was back in basic training knocking out hundreds of sit-ups and push-ups. I was back to being capable of bearing the weight of anything that I might encounter at work.

Basketball

One afternoon when I finished lifting weights, I discovered a group of men playing basketball at mid-life. There were roughly a dozen guys of ages ranging from my own into their 60s as part of an Over 40 pickup game, so I asked about the rules and whether I might be able to play. Up until that point, my routine at the gym was nomadic and I really hadn't made any friends since getting divorced, so I saw the game as an opportunity to potentially find some camaraderie and have a little fun running around the court rather than the monotony of jogging on a cardio machine.

Basketball has always been my favorite sport to watch since I was a kid in Michigan rooting for the Detroit Pistons to beat Michael Jordan and the Chicago Bulls. As a player, I always looked up to Isiah Thomas because of his shorter height and fierce competitiveness. In his honor, I always wore #11 when playing sports. While hustle served me well as a defender in basketball, I was never coordinated or skilled enough to be much of an offensive threat. It'd been over 25 years since I'd played on my middle school's team, so I questioned whether I'd be able to keep up with guys who'd clearly been playing for a long time, but one day I was feeling spry and decided to give it a go. I fumbled passes, missed layups, and fell enough to leave bruises; but everyone seemed to encourage my enthusiasm and gave me tips for improving. Clearly I had a long way to go to hold my own on the court, but I was hooked.

For the next several months, I worked on shooting before lifting weights and always arrived early for game days so I could practice. Games were scheduled every Monday and Thursday, so I began planning my bartending schedule to open instead of close on those nights. Playing every week introduced me to a circle of people who'd known each other for years, and in a small way I finally found some camaraderie beyond the bartending community when they let me join them. These folks were fairly accomplished lawyers, medical doctors, executives, etc., and there I was a service industry guy barely scraping by. However, one's profession doesn't mean anything on the court–it's just about your skill, effort, and sportsmanship–so no one took much interest in how I was making a living at the time.

I was working almost every day to make ends meet, but I still made a commitment to take care of my physical health. I'd either work out before or after a shift, and the pattern revolutionized the way I was feeling. My routine became running via basketball on Mondays and Thursdays, lifting weights on Tuesdays and Fridays, taking yoga classes on Wednesdays and Sundays, and swimming on Saturdays. It's a cycle that I still go through every week, and has helped me not only strengthen my body, but also provided an opportunity to start socializing with people again. I'd reached a point where I could finally start thinking about caring for someone beside myself again.

119

CHAPTER 8

THE POWER OF THE
WEST HIGHLAND TERRIER

It's hard to find companionship as a bartender. After all, it's a job with a schedule the opposite of traditional work. When the average person is done at the office and fighting traffic on the way home, we're just clocking in and will be going until the streets are basically empty. Sure, shopping and running errands in the afternoon when places aren't as crowded is a minor benefit of the hours, but meeting up with friends or family becomes a scheduling nightmare. Holidays and weekends are when you make the most tips, so you're rarely available to socialize. You sometimes have drinks with your fellow bartenders, but they're just as unavailable.

Finding a partner that accepts such a schedule is difficult. When you get home in the middle of the night, the last thing you want to do is talk. You just want something to numb the pain of being on your feet all day and calm your mind. Rest is what you need. The sort of pattern of closing the bar where you work, going to another bar, and then going to sleep at 3am before waking up at noon like a teenager becomes your daily ritual until you find a way to break the cycle. For me, the solution came in the form of having a best friend waiting at home–a dog that's always happy to see me, doesn't require having a conversation, and is always looking out for my welfare.

○ ○ ○

Growing up in the military made it difficult to have a pet. I always wanted a dog like many of my friends, but we were constantly on the move. For a short period of time while we were assigned to California, my father trained a hulking black lab for hunting. He was aptly named Moose for his size and his tail was strong enough to knock me over. When we would go for walks, he'd pick out the largest branch in the forest and bring it back like a prize with the muscles in his neck fully clenched. He was trained to retrieve ducks and the compulsion was deeply embedded in his genetics. Moose wasn't really a house pet and could look intimidating, but he had a sweet disposition. When we eventually had to move again, I recall that my father gave him to a kind UPS driver who said she had a large fenced property where he could exercise and it seemed like the right place for him to go.

After I graduated high school in Germany, my father gave me an opportunity to go somewhere in Europe for a long weekend as a gift before I started college. Being of

Scottish-Irish descent, I decided to travel to Scotland for the first time. The flight arrived in Glasgow and I took a train to a bed and breakfast I could barely afford in a small town called Loch Lomond. The lush green landscape and dreary weather immediately reminded me of Michigan; which is likely why so many immigrants from the region moved to the Great Lakes. I loved spending the mornings reading, the afternoons hiking the trails surrounding the lake, and visiting the public houses for pints and Scotch in the evening. However, my favorite part of the trip was meeting all of the little white dogs with their wiry hair and smiling faces patrolling the streets and resting in pubs like the country's unofficial mascot: the West Highland Terrier.

Westies were originally bred for the specific purpose of tracking down small rodents by burrowing into holes and using their carrot-shaped tail like a handle to pull them back out. I saw myself in their sense of loyalty and expressive character. They're small in stature, but intrepid–just like me–so it was love at first sight. The trip was one of the happiest moments I've ever experienced, and Westies came to represent the sort of warm-hearted feeling of the memories. Unfortunately, I was on the way to military school and on track to serve as an officer who would have to be on the move just like my childhood, so my dream of becoming a Westie parent was put on hold for nearly a decade.

○ ○ ○

When I left the military, high on my list of priorities was finally settling down and starting a family like my friends, but raising a puppy instead of a child. Being a parent of sorts was something I wanted to experience. On the other hand, my spouse approached the subject with trepidation. He'd always been a cat owner, and there were too many unknowns for how a dog might throw off the balance of our homelife. Some of his friends went as far as to warn that we'd be flirting with breaking up (even after five years of marriage) if we adopted a dog. Hence, my husband came up with requirements/demands for any potential addition to our family: they had to be able to go to the bathroom in a box akin to litter training, they couldn't chase the cats, and they needed to be quiet. It was a tall order for a puppy–much like the unrealistic expectations that were placed on me as a spouse.

One morning when reading the local newspaper, I found an ad for Westie puppies and we decided to go meet the litter. The breeder was a kind woman in her 60s with curly black hair wearing a knitted sweater and distressed jeans who lived twenty miles from Phoenix, so she brought the puppies to a hotel room for people to meet. When we arrived, there were already two other couples cooing over five cotton-white siblings in a makeshift pen wrestling with each other for attention. Meanwhile, their brother, the runt of the litter, was on the other side of the fenced area looking back at us with eyes glinting like black marbles. The name I had always wanted for a dog was Quincy, after the doctor in the television series, and I had finally found him.

As I've been told, nothing prepares you for parenthood–you just try to do the best you can. When we adopted Quincy he was small enough to fit in my hand, and the responsibility for his life immediately kicked in. I can only imagine how overwhelmed my young parents must have felt when I was born. We knew nothing about how to nurture a puppy, keep him healthy, and teach him where to go to the bathroom, much less condition him to meet all of my husband's expectations. The first night he was home he whimpered for his mother like a child with colic keeping us awake. For the first few weeks, we kept him in a kennel to separate him from the cats who curiously studied him from afar. Everyone's routines had been upended by our new addition, and our lives would never be the same.

Both being teachers, you'd think we'd be good at training an animal, but our experience with college students really didn't translate, so we eventually sought help from a trainer. A man in his 50s with a cropped black beard and denim jacket arrived in a truck with an older German shepherd who patiently stood by as a model; hardly batting an eye at our rambunctious little guy. It wasn't so much about training our dog as it was training us to be consistent and paying attention to patterns in behavior. The trainer taught us the power of eye contact, shortening the length of commands for better understanding, and positive reinforcement. He taught us more in one session than anything we had read or watched on training.

Little by little, Quincy grew from a puppy into a dog and we learned the role of being good parents. I trained him how to go to the bathroom on paper in a plastic box until he was old enough to scratch the door when he needed to go outside, but being quiet and not chasing the cats were a bridge too far for a precocious terrier. We quickly discovered how bright and vocal his breed can be with varying tones that function like words. *Stranger danger! Bird landing! Throw my toy! Let me out!* His vocabulary approximates a kindergartner and is just as unfiltered as my habitually operating mouth as a teenager. It's fascinating how dogs take on the temperament of their owners like children mirror the behavior of their parents. I guess that makes me a Westie, too.

In the final months of my marriage, my relationship had deteriorated to the point that I was closer to Quincy than my husband. He was my constant companion and protector. In moments when staring into our pool (that we owed tens of thousands of dollars in debt) considering my future, he always kept watch over me. When I would drift away in thought, he would place a paw on my leg to bring me back to the present moment. When I was ready to give up, his presence reminded me of my responsibility to take care of him. In many ways, he's the reason I'm still here.

After what would turn out to be the final argument with my husband, I locked myself in the office and slept on the floor with Quincy burrowed beside me. I wrestled all night trying to decide what I would do next until I awoke to the lock of the room being picked. I grabbed the handle and opened the door to the surprise of my husband, who said, "I just wanted to make sure you didn't hurt yourself." In that moment, I realized he knew I was suicidal and was willing to wait until morning–to leave me for dead rather than help me. There was no salvaging our relationship, so I packed a suitcase with Quincy watching, picked him up to hold like when he was a puppy, and whispered in his ear that I'd be back for him.

Weeks later, when I was able to find a small apartment, my lawyer arranged for me to be able to pick up my remaining items. I sorely missed Quincy and couldn't wait to bring him home, but arrived to find that my husband had taken him away in the name of *community property*. My son. Stolen. The act confirmed that I had made the right decision to leave, and I've never doubted my choice since. However, staring at a custody battle that would take an indefinite amount of time and financial resources that I simply didn't have, I knew the right thing for Quincy was to stay in the home we'd made for him. I hadn't cried in a long time, but experiencing his loss was overwhelming in a way that I can only associate with my mother having to give up custody of me. Not taking him with me is one of my greatest regrets.

○ ○ ○

It would take over a year and a half until our divorce proceedings reached a point of arbitration. By that time, I'd been forced into accepting unemployment assistance due to the brewery where I was working, like so many hospitality establishments, closing without hope of reopening. One of my only sources of support came from the Arizona Bartender's Association, which set up a grocery donation program that offered a free bag of groceries including dry goods like flour, rice, and beans for anyone in need. The bag lasted me nearly a month until my aunt and uncle realized how little I was living on and began dividing their wholesale groceries into a delivery for me every other week. Moreover, I had to ask for a loan from my family to keep paying my lawyer since my credit was nearly maxed out trying to make ends meet. Adopting another dog had been out of the question until our divorce finally reached a settlement and I was able to pay off my debts.

As part of starting the next chapter of my life, reaching closure with my divorce and letting go of the trauma of losing Quincy, the first investment I made with the remaining funds from the settlement was to respond to a social media posting for a litter of Westies available for adoption. In reply, I received a request for two references and scheduled time for an interview like a job application. It made me a bit nervous about the sort of questions they would ask, but it was good to know that they cared enough about the puppies to make sure they found the right home. As it turned out, they mainly wanted to ask my friends the type of person I am so they could consider which puppy would be the right match–all without meeting in person.

A few days later, I received pictures of an adorable Westie only eight weeks old who looked exactly like Quincy when he was so young he fit in the palm of my hand. At the time, I was periodically giving film lectures for extra money and happened to be presenting a talk on Wes Anderson's *The Royal Tenenbaums* to a group of seniors at a retirement community. I'd been wrestling with finding the right name before bringing my bundle of joy home and while I was taking notes rewatching the movie the name of the family's dog immediately struck me as the perfect fit: Buckley. Not unlike the ending of the film when the Tenenbaums adopt another dog after the loss of their pet, I knew that picking up Buckley was the start of a new chapter. I was ready to be a father again and start rebuilding the family surrounding me.

STAGE 5
MAINTENANCE

Only through great commitment is great change truly possible. During the maintenance stage, a person is working hard to prevent recovery relapse. They're also keeping up the lifestyle changes they made, like getting regular exercise, recreational activities, paying attention to sleep, hygiene, and attending support groups. They don't feel the urge to relapse as frequently as people in the action stage, so their confidence grows and they truly believe in their ability to move forward with their lives.

The maintenance stage is so immense that it encompasses the entirety of the "late" recovery phase. While there are many physical actions that can be taken to avoid falling into old habits, true maintenance is about using your newfound perspective to explore the root of your need for recovery.

131

CHAPTER 9

THE SUM OF THE PARTS

I lost my sense of community when I left my marriage. Even after knowing me for over a decade, many people I considered close friends and even family members disappeared from my life like they'd been part of an illusion. It took years of building relationships between my husband's constellation of academic colleagues, friends of a different generation, and associates in the art world with my fellow veterans, peers at the beginning of their careers, and classmates living across the globe—not to mention our contrasting family backgrounds.

My husband grew up in the Lutheran church as the son of a pastor with two parents, a built-in support system, consistency in school, and siblings close in age. Oppositely, religion was never an influence in my family, my parents divorced at an early age, I regularly had to change schools, and my sisters largely grew up separately from me. There were numerous intersections of our interests and experiences that served as the foundation for our identity as a couple; however, when we separated I was left with trying to reconstruct my own as an individual.

In my mind, our personalities are the sum of our experiences with different communities. In his book *No Bad Parts*, Richard Schwartz describes these aspects, or multiple dimensions, of our personalities as Internal Family Systems (IFS) that can be examined through "parts work." Schwartz came up with the idea for IFS more than 40 years ago when he was a family therapist treating adolescents with bulimia. His patients told him about different *parts* of themselves that were interfering with their treatment, like "The Critic" who would make them feel worthless and alone. Essentially, our minds are not one-dimensional. Schwartz says, "We all have multiple perspectives within." For example, people often identify parts such as the self, protector, manager, and exile. Some parts tend to dominate our lives, while others are more hidden. IFS teaches a process to embrace all your parts, bring them into balance, and find a sense of wholeness.

Once I read and learned more about this form of therapy, I began to consider the different parts of myself that are anchored in the communities I've belonged to in my life and the feelings associated with them. The wanderlust of growing up as a traveler, the insecurity of being raised in and serving in the military, the determination of always seeking achievement and being a people pleaser, and the defensive nature of guarding my identity as a gay man were the parts of myself I needed to work on.

The Traveler
(The Self)

They say the apple doesn't fall far from the tree, but my upbringing was more like being plucked at an unripe age and shipped to a market overseas. Since my father was assigned to Japan, and my mother remained where I was born in Michigan, I split time between the two by being shuttled on flights back and forth from Asia. Saying goodbye to my parents before boarding flights was an act of emotional scarring that was reopened whenever we went to the airport, so I can only imagine how painful it must have been for them to repeat the words back to me and watch the image of their son walking down the gangway. Staying in one place was never an option. In turn, setting foot onto an airplane for a day's worth of travel on the way to a foreign country defined my upbringing and taught me at an early age not to fear the unknown–but embrace the opportunity to see more of the world as a traveler.

Starting school overseas exposed me to a completely different landscape, language, and set of cultural practices that expanded my view of the world. I remember spending days at the beach while my father went scuba diving, chasing lizards outside our apartment with my friends, watching all the television shows featuring ninjas and samurai, and the many sensory experiences that I'll never forget. The sweet taste of melon candy. The pungent smell of seafood markets. The peculiar sight of people eating live tadpoles with a spoon. The calming sound of ocean waves. The sharp touch of assembling pieces of toy robots. And the feeling of hands patting my blonde hair for good luck. Learning the norms and traditions of Japanese culture taught me at an early age that just because something is different from what you've come to know doesn't make it wrong. More often than not, it can further inform options you may have never considered.

○ ○ ○

By the time I started high school in Germany in 1996, I'd traveled extensively around the United States between my parents' assignments in the military and road trips to visit places like National Parks. Growing up on the move taught me that change was inevitable and not to fear it. I grew comfortable being uncomfortable and it gave me the strength to move past the typical anxieties of encountering unfamiliar situations. Moving from Texas to Europe was daunting as a teenager who'd never been there before, but I knew that my father and I would be living in a military community where many of the other students had repeatedly been in the same situation and we all knew how to adapt to our surroundings.

Within a few weeks, I picked up some German phrases, learned how to navigate their transportation systems, and started getting to know people. Joining the soccer team helped me quickly make friends. Matches on the weekends took place across Germany as well as in other countries like Italy, Belgium, and England. Moreover, my father became an active member of the base's ski club, so we went on numerous excursions across France, Austria, and Switzerland, where I learned how to snowboard on the back slopes of the Matterhorn. By the end of my first year of high school, I'd seen more of Europe than most Americans will in a lifetime.

I can remember returning home to Michigan for the summer and showing my family all the pictures I'd taken on disposable cameras that reflected the inspiration of being exposed to so many different cultures. One of my cousins actually commented on a photo of me in front of the Eiffel Tower that they thought it was just a setting from a movie, and in a way that's what the experience felt like. I was finding my way in the world and I knew that travel would continue to be a driving force throughout my development.

○ ○ ○

When I joined the Speech and Debate team in college, tournaments took us all over the country nearly every other weekend. The season lasted the entire academic year, and I competed for all four years, so by the time I graduated my count of states visited was already at 48–with Alaska and Maine to follow on vacations with my husband. As I transitioned out of the military and into graduate school, I began coaching speech and debate and maintained the same rigorous travel schedule. As a former coach himself, my husband still maintained a role in the community by running an international tournament in alternating countries every year. In turn, we started a routine of traveling to an international destination during Spring Break every year to destinations like Vienna, Prague, Lima, Buenos Aires, Tokyo, and Seoul.

Eventually, when my husband retired, I took over leadership as the president of the organization, the International Forensics Association, as an opportunity to give the experience of travel, often for the first time abroad, to thousands of undergraduate students. Helping host the tournament for 20 years was one of the greatest acts of service in my life, and I'm proud of the many contributions we made to the speech and debate community–including founding a scholarship in my name to help students participate in the tournament.

○ ○ ○

In a surreal return to Germany, my first assignment for the University of Maryland's Global Campus was to teach where I went to high school on an army fort in Wiesbaden. The posters I'd seen on the bulletin board advertising college courses now had my name attached to them. It's powerful how travel can sometimes take us back to the same place, but with a different set of eyes. I was no longer a teenager with a narrow focus on my studies and friends; I'd matured into an adult who embraced the beauty of the city's architecture, natural spas, and historic downtown that was largely spared of bombing during World War II. All of my sensory memories as a teenager came rushing back. The herbaceous flavor of Frankfurter Grüne Soße on schnitzel. The stench of the many people who don't use deodorant. The spectacle of Christmas markets. The sounds of airplane engines roaring over our apartment building. The weight of a liter beer stein in my hand. And the strength of the bonds with German friends from my childhood who'd found a way to stay in touch with my father and me over the years.

However, leaving my German friends again for subsequent assignments in Spain and England reminded me how conditioned I'd become at an early age to accept the eventuality of having to leave loved ones behind. I finally started to realize how it was just as hard for people I'd created strong bonds with to let me go as it was for me to have to leave them. When I was growing up, the internet didn't exist yet and maintaining friendships by writing letters and long distance phone calls never lasted, but by the time I was in high school email helped me stay in touch with my friends living across the globe. Once social media arrived when I was in college, the ability to stay in connection with anyone who wanted to follow posts and see how my life was going was at the touch of my fingers. While I understand its downsides, social media that's now readily available on smart phones has allowed me to replace the feeling of absence I'd always struggled with by the feeling of presence (at least from afar) in my friends' lives.

As much as my husband enjoyed living abroad for the first several months, it was difficult for him to adapt to not being surrounded by his support system and leaving the comfort of routines he'd created over decades of living and working in Phoenix. It's one thing to visit a place as a tourist for a few days, but another to be immersed in a different society where you don't speak the language or understand the cultural norms. Compounded with my work schedule, it must've felt isolating in a way that I'd grown numb to recognizing. For the first time in our marriage, my husband was reliant on me for navigating us through the challenges of living abroad and I started to acknowledge some of the responsibility my father must've felt raising me in unfamiliar environments for us both.

Unfortunately, the longer we stayed overseas the more it stressed my husband, so we made the decision to return to Arizona. Doing so meant an end to our traveling and a step back in my career as we reverted to the security of the life we'd built in the desert. In retrospect, it would've been the healthiest decision for us both if we had brought an end to our codependency and decided to allow our paths to part, but it wasn't a truth either of us was willing to admit at the time. I was a traveler wedded to a tourist and it would take years for me to accept that nothing I could do would change that difference. There's a part of me that will always be the boy walking down the gangway with a backpack filled with toys and books–the apple being shipped away–moving on to the next adventure on my own.

The Warrior
(The Protector)

I'm from a rural part of Michigan called Ionia that's best known for its county prisons, tractor supply, and brick-lined mainstreet. The men in my family either joined the military, ended up working for General Motors, or both. My paternal grandfather fought in the Korean War as a Marine, my maternal grandfather and uncles served in the Navy, my mother served in the Army, and my father in the Air Force (he enlisted when I was only a few years old). Being from the Great Lakes and a family of outdoorsmen, I grew up around weapons long before I joined the military. Moreover, my father wrestled in high school, and my mother boxed in community college, so they taught me how to protect myself and fight at an early age–qualities that were reinforced in the warrior culture of being raised in the military community.

○ ○ ○

I started high school with the intention of proving myself, not only as a student, but as a young adult who was prepared to take on the responsibilities that the veterans in my family had accepted before me. I wanted to be part of a legacy of service, and the best way I saw to start that journey was to enroll in JROTC. Competing in sports cultivated a part of me that strives for achievement, and the sense of challenge associated with a program to prepare for joining the military that intimidated most students was motivating for me. There's nothing that drives me more than overcoming adversity–particularly when someone says I can't accomplish something–so I set out to be the best JROTC cadet I could possibly be for General H. H. Arnold High School's Wiesbaden Warriors.

The program at our school was sponsored by the U.S. Air Force, so classes centered on aerospace history and technology. In our freshman year, we learned how to properly wear uniforms, march in formations, and respect the military's rank structure. There was a focus on civic duty and volunteerism that resonated with me, so I started spending nearly all my time involved with service opportunities. Moreover, our unit had an honor guard and drill team that represented the highest level of dedication. Members raised the American flag every morning, presented the colors when "The Star-Spangled Banner" was played at local events, and competed with other Air Force programs as well as all the Army and Navy units from all over Europe.

While seniority played a role in earning your rank, what I loved the most about JROTC was how progression was largely driven by merit. Accomplishments were acknowledged with ribbons and medals, so for anyone motivated by achievement there was a visual way to distinguish yourself from other cadets. Volunteering was the fastest way to earn your first ribbon, so I started working at our unit's snack stand during the lunch period selling instant noodles, soda, and candy. In retrospect, it was my introduction to the hospitality industry and fitting that the first award pinned to my uniform was the Service Ribbon.

The people-pleaser in me, particularly for male role models, subconsciously fueled my determination to gain attention for my efforts. By the spring semester, everyone knew that I was dedicated, reliable, and a natural leader who emerged as one of the most skilled and disciplined cadets in our corps. After a year of learning how to spin a rifle, handle a sabre, and perform special ceremonies; I was fortunate to be a part of our drill team winning the Sabre Exhibition event at the European Championships. Combined with my academic performance and over 100 volunteer hours, I earned my first medal and was promoted to be an officer at the start of my sophomore year–something that was normally reserved for upperclassmen. I can still recall the awards ceremony at the end of the school year, and how one of the seniors had earned a scholarship to the U.S Air Force Academy equivalent to $250,000 at the time. I really didn't have a clear direction for what I'd do after high school until that moment. I immediately became determined to achieve the same level of recognition as well as save my parents the financial burden of paying for college.

Neither of my parents ever pressured me to take the path of joining the military or attending college; nor did they place any expectations of me other than being a person of integrity. Dedicating the majority of my time toward JROTC was deeply rooted in the challenge of proving people wrong–even if no one ever actually expressed such a challenge. I was primarily motivated by competing with myself, so set out to take on more responsibility in my second year by running the snack stand and serving as the Executive Officer for our drill team. I also joined a sister organization with a similar rank structure related to JROTC called the Civil Air Patrol (CAP) that focused on developing pilot skills and served a contingency role in search and rescue missions.

Another year passed with more recognition and promotions, so I doubled-down on my goal of earning a nomination to the Air Force Academy in my junior year by completing a summer boot camp sponsored by Army JROTC as a distinguished graduate, serving as the Commander of the drill team that would go on to win the overall European championship, and earning the highest rank in CAP across all the detachments in Europe. By this time, the chest of my uniform was stacked with honors and I came to the realization that I'd accomplished more than I could've possibly dreamed as a freshman. The only remaining role for me in JROTC was to serve as our unit's Commander. Unfortunately, another student was chosen to give them a leadership opportunity. I saw the oversight as an insult that ultimately motivated my decision to pivot my focus toward my academic performance and leadership opportunities in other extracurricular activities.

Distancing from JROTC in my senior year, I chose to invest my energy in student government, joining Model United Nations, serving as a regent for the International Student Leadership Institute, traveling to the National Youth Leadership Summit in Washington D.C., and taking Advanced Placement courses. I ended up applying to roughly a dozen colleges (mostly based on their sports teams since I really didn't know much about higher education at the time), but my goal was still to earn an appointment to the Air Force Academy. My application must have looked impressive except for one thing: my mediocre performance on the math portion of the SAT. Since the admissions office would allow you to take the test multiple times and use your top scores in verbal and math, I ended up taking the test four times. My verbal scores came back high each time, but my math scores were always middling, so it was crushing when I received a thin envelope from the

Air Force Academy with a brief note of rejection. I can still vividly recall unlocking the combination of our mailbox, seeing the official sender, knowing that acceptance letters came in larger packages with booklets, and breaking down in tears. As a teenager, it felt like my life had been cut short. While I received a few acceptance letters in the weeks that followed, being rejected from the school that had served as a beacon to me for years gave me my first taste of depression. I began retreating from activities and hunkered down in my room listening to sad music and playing video games as a distraction.

Then came a letter that I wasn't expecting: a scholarship offer from an organization called the Falcon Foundation to attend military school with their academic mentoring to secure an assured appointment to the Air Force Academy the following year. My backup option was to join the ROTC unit at the University of Michigan, where I probably would've had a much healthier college experience, but of course I chose to accept the more difficult challenge. I decided the next step of proving myself after high school was to accept the opportunity of enrolling at New Mexico Military Institute (NMMI).

○ ○ ○

Why New Mexico? The traveler in me was excited by the thought of living someplace new and with more days of sunshine than Germany. However, the real reason behind my decision–which embarrassingly demonstrates my immaturity as a teenager–was that I was a huge fan of *The X-Files* television series and NMMI was located in the rumored location of alien sightings in Roswell. As disciples of the show will understand, I wanted to believe.

Prior to the start of Basic Training and a grueling year of Army ROTC indoctrination, I flew from Germany to Michigan to spend the last weeks of the summer and my adolescence with my mother. While it was wonderful to celebrate graduating from high school with my family and having a break before starting college, a doubt had begun to set in whether I could make it through yet another test of my dedication. Not because of the intensity of the environment or discipline required, but because I'd started to question whether I was gay, and it terrified me. I knew that if I ever acted on those thoughts then I'd be dishonorably drummed out of NMMI and shame my family; but I never spoke to anyone about the way I was feeling. I'd stay awake at night worrying so much that suicide began to creep into my mind for the first time. I knew where the weapons were in my mother's home and how to use them. It would be so much easier to quit than continue, but the idea of hurting my family and friends outweighed what I viewed as a selfish act, so I boarded my flight to Albuquerque with the perseverance to keep advancing toward my goal of graduating from the Air Force Academy.

Awaiting me in New Mexico was a shuttle bus that took incoming cadets to the campus in Roswell–a tightly knit cluster of sepia-colored gothic buildings sequestered in the high plains of the Chihuahuan Desert. When we arrived, I was disarmed by how welcoming the staff were as they walked us through a series of stations where they shaved our heads, provided the items and clothes we'd need for their version of Basic Training, and escorted us to our rooms to meet our roommates and unpack. The whole process was designed to get everyone to let their guard down before the upperclassmen knocked our doors down the following morning at 6am and our initiation began.

While there were retired veterans who served as supervisors, the vast majority of the training was run by students–many of whom were sent to NMMI for one behavioral issue or another. A number of cadets were there because they were given a choice by a judge, so you can imagine how they conducted themselves when given an opportunity to haze underclassmen. Moreover, the experience was unique because the high school and junior college students were blended together in the different platoons, so the power dynamic of having high school students berate us was hard to tolerate. Thankfully, there was nothing particularly taxing about the training itself that I hadn't been through before and I was in great physical shape, so my worries about being able to hack it were quickly forgotten.

After a few weeks, the training staff came to respect me and I was recruited for NMMI's Ranger Challenge Team—essentially a Varsity sport between different Army ROTC programs in an annual competition. The events included an M-16 proficiency check, a written warrior skills test, a physical fitness test (push-ups, sit-ups and a two-mile run), a first aid test, an obstacle course, a grenade assault course, a day and night orienteering course, as well as a 10-kilometer ruck march in full battle gear. Practices were every weekday morning starting at 0600 hours before classes, which made for grueling days, but I was intent on proving that I was ready for the challenge.

Most importantly, joining the team helped me make friends and find camaraderie living away from home for the first time. Once I learned the skills necessary for the competition and acclimated to the demands of practices, I started to feel a sense of strength that propelled me through the rest of the school year. My academic courses weren't particularly difficult by comparison, and the team also had tutors in different subjects, so I was able to focus on improving my math scores—which eventually met the standards for the Air Force Academy. In retrospect, although we didn't place very high at the annual competition, joining the team was the best choice I could've made for preparing for the next stop in my journey: leaving the desert of New Mexico for the front range of the Rockies in Colorado.

○ ○ ○

They say the only thing more difficult than getting into a service academy is graduating from one. By this point you can start to understand what it took for me to earn my seat on the bus that drove us from the registration building of the U.S. Air Force Academy to the entrance ramp of the campus with a phrase that welcomes new recruits with a line from Samuel Walter Foss that reads BRING ME MEN like the infamous WORK SETS YOU FREE message to those sentenced to concentration camps. The initiation ritual begins the moment you step off the bus to find large black blocks with white footprints painted on them to arrange everyone in formation while the upperclassmen get in the face of each recruit barking insults at any shortcoming they can find–things I'd grown numb to from my experience at NMMI, but still exhausting when you have to endure them on a daily basis.

The first day of Basic Cadet Training (BCT), or "Beast," is largely marching from various stations across the campus to shave your head, pick up your uniforms, issue your rifle, receive vaccinations, set up your mailbox, and get your room assignment. Once you meet your roommates (three to a 15' x 15' space) your first task is to clean it without any products or tools. You dust and even act like a vacuum cleaning the floor with your hands, make your bed with specific measurements and angles, fold all your clothes in a precise way, meticulously arrange your toiletries, and start to realize how hellish the days ahead will be. When it's time for inspection, the training staff latch on to the smallest of details and use it as an excuse to upturn the mattresses, empty everything onto the floor, and berate you for being a failure. It's a rite of passage that they've all been through, and they all want to make it just as bad–if not worse–than what they experienced.

At meals, you learn a technique called *squares* to lift bites directly into the air to be level with your mouth before you bring the utensil to your mouth. You only get seven chews per bite and the training staff love to count them for you so they can issue any variety of punishments at the table. The worst for me was having to lift your knees off the ground to touch the bottom of the table while you ate. Failure to follow protocol essentially meant you'd barely eat, so I started to dread what was usually my favorite part of the day.

You're issued a small booklet called *Contrails* that serves as your Bible for learning about military history, ranks, procedures, and anything trivial the authors could stuff into a pocket reference you carry at all times for the entire year. Whenever there's downtime or you have to wait in line for an appointment, you have to take the book out and memorize sections that you're quizzed on daily. Quotations from the book become so ingrained that graduates can all recite the most meaningful ones to them decades later.

After the first three weeks on campus acclimating to an altitude of 7,258 feet, the second half of BCT is spent living outdoors in Jack's Valley. The march into the valley signals the transition from being indoctrinated into the standards of the Academy to proving yourself in the field as worthy of being part of what's referred to as a Warrior Culture. You learn how to build a camp, go through marksmanship training, complete obstacle courses, go through combat simulations with gunfire and grenade explosions, and are essentially pushed until you reach a breaking point. When your body physically collapses or you have an emotional breakdown, will you find a way to keep going or give up? The training staff are there to test whether you're a warrior or a quitter–and they love nothing more than driving someone to drop out rather than wasting their time on someone who will only end up letting their fellow soldiers down. The stakes were far beyond high school or junior college; we were being prepared to handle life or death situations.

While I was more than prepared for the first half of BCT and fared well in Jack's Valley, escaping being what they call "broken" was impossible. There were points in the physical training when my body involuntarily shook and my muscles gave out from stress positions, my gut would gag from being forced to chug entire canteens of water, my eyes were blinded from tear gas, and moments my mind didn't recall from blacking out. Thoughts of suicide returned from the constant harrasment and lingering questions in my subconscious of why I was subjecting myself to such punishment, but my willpower pushed me to keep going. Over 5% of our class didn't make it to the end of Basic Training. The staff had accomplished their mission and decided that we were ready to march back to campus where the upperclassmen were waiting in the dorms for their turn to decide whether we were worthy of joining their ranks.

The grueling process of being "recognized" at service academies takes the entire academic year. It begins when you return from Jack's Valley and meet the rest of the cadets assigned to the one of 40 different squadrons you're in. The campus has two dormitories that are each six-stories high that are divided into blocks of rooms for each squadron. Freshmen are referred to as Doolies, 4-degrees, or SMACKS (Soldiers Minus Ability, Coordination, or Knowledge). An active duty officer as well as enlisted mentor have offices within the squadrons as supervisors, but upperclassmen are responsible for all of the training and operations.

After you're broken down in BCT, members of your squadron start to rebuild you to their standards through daily physical, mental, and emotional conditioning. Every morning starts before sunrise with PT, followed by an afternoon accountability formation during the lunch period, knowledge tests from *Contrails*, and the immense amount of homework from having a full course load of six classes for 18 credits.

There's never enough time by design. It's like being thrown into the deep end of a pool and trying to learn how to swim while the lifeguard stands by yelling at you for not knowing better. You either learn how to adapt or drown. That's how you prove your character.

A month into my first semester, I was at the optometrist with my eyes dilated for what felt like an hour waiting for the doctor, but she never returned. A nurse entered and told me that the Pentagon had been attacked and the doctor's husband was assigned there, so my appointment would need to be rescheduled. I found my way to the lobby to see every television tuned into the news showing a plane crashing into the World Trade Center. My eyes had never been so open. A siren suddenly sounded, signalling everyone to return to their rooms because the campus was being locked down for security, so I ran back to our squadron in the blinding sun. The halls were crowded with upperclassmen venting their rage. Cadets shouting, "We're going kill the mother fuckers that did this!" still echoes in my mind. In that moment, we all realized that our training was no longer an exercise in discipline—our nation was going to war.

The events of 9/11 added a level of intensity that pushed the boundaries of what was permissible in our training. I'd been sucker-punched in the stomach at NMMI after making a sarcastic comment during an inspection, but that was the only time I can recall someone hazing me in a physical way until an upperclassman pinned me to a wall during a training session at the Air Force Academy. I pushed back and told them to *Get your fucking hands off me!* and it caught the attention of other cadets who paused what was going on. I complained to the Officer in Charge of our squadron and the upperclassmen received a warning. After that point, I had a target on my back and the training staff made sure I regretted speaking up.

Weeks later, in an event that I still view as retribution, I was accused of an honor violation for allegedly cheating on one of our regular knowledge quizzes about current events and assigned sections of *Contrails* we were supposed to memorize. The quizzes were typically 10 questions on a scratch sheet of paper and weren't part of any performance record. Their purpose was designed for us to fail and serve as a rationale for additional training. There was no motivation for anyone to cheat because we knew we'd get "beat" (pushed to the point of physical collapse) by the upperclassmen anyway. The accusation came from my using a pencil to cross out two answers before the end of the quiz and correcting them. Despite my explanation that my pencil didn't have an eraser (because I'd chewed it off out of returning anxiety), the cadet proctoring the exam insisted that I face an Honor Board to decide whether I should stay or be expelled.

The process of facing a trial by 12 of my peers was intimidating and the potential repercussions were so terrifying that I sought counsel from the Legal Assistance Office. I was assigned a lawyer who rolled his eyes and explained that these sorts of allegations happen all the time. He asked me about the details of the situation and drafted around 10 questions that he recommended I ask in my defense. When the board convened, the proctor of the exam never even attended the hearing and my questions went unanswered. After about 15 minutes of deliberation while I anxiously waited with my friends outside the boardroom for the decision, they called me back in to announce that I'd been found innocent. A wave of relief washed over me that was briefly celebrated until the bitterness of having to go through such an unnecessary trial set in. My idealism about the Academy shifted to cynicism and my attitude was never the same after the incident.

Disillusioned in the same way I'd grown in high school, I lost faith in leadership and the motivation to prove myself to them, so I shifted my focus to other interests and goals. As I'll detail in a subsequent section, my life began to revolve around scholarship as an English major and member of the Speech and Debate team. I avoided being in my squadron as much as possible by attending office hours with my professors, hunkering down in the library, and traveling to tournaments. The upperclassmen loathed me and made a point of ridiculing me every chance they got, but I knew that my mind and body were tough enough to make it to the end of the first year. After being recognized, we were thankfully reassigned to a new squadron so we wouldn't hold grudges against the cadets who trained us as freshmen.

Summers were divided into three blocks of three week sessions. Unfortunately, I failed Electromagnetic Physics and had to retake the course over the summer, so that took up the first session. The next was spent in skydiving training with one of my roommates who went on to join the Wings of Blue Parachute Team. After completing five freefall jumps, I earned my parachute wings and advanced to the third session that required us to return to Jack's Valley for Cadet Survival Training (CST). My parents both enjoyed camping, so I already knew most of the techniques like building a fire and killing a rabbit like they taught us in the first half of CST, but the evasion and resistance portion consisted of Prisoner of War simulations where we were forced to lie face down for hours while being interrogated and given only a cup of rice a day. By the time we returned to campus, we all smelled disgusting and were ravenous. I remember being so exhausted and caked in mud that I took a chair into the shower followed by eating three hamburgers in the chow hall like a competitive eater.

A few days later while we were all packing to move to our newly assigned squadrons to begin our sophomore year, I was told by an upperclassman to report to our Officer in Charge's office. As a freshman, I rarely had any interaction with him, so I had no idea what to expect. I reported with a salute and was told to stand at ease. He told me he knew I was on the Speech and Debate team and there was some bad news: my debate partner, Nate Hewitt, had passed away after getting in a car accident driving late at night on the way to see his girlfriend in Utah. He was only 22. We didn't take many pictures prior to the advent of smartphones, but I have a team photo of us both that I hold on to in his memory–Nate with his beaming smile and me with a smirk wishing I could share his positive outlook on a life that was cut short far too early.

The events of going through an Honor Board and mourning Nate's loss completely changed my perspective going into my sophomore year. I finally realized that I'd burnt out on proving myself as a soldier and wanted to dedicate my time to more intellectual challenges. Being transferred to a new squadron was a perfect opportunity to reinvent myself. When it came time to apply for job assignments within the squadron, I chose to bypass the interview process and run for the only role that required being elected: Honor Representative. After I shared my story and explained how I wanted to help prevent other cadets from going through the same situation I'd experienced, I was unanimously elected.

Moreover, all of the squadrons were divided into four Groups within the overall Cadet Wing, and I won an additional election to represent our Group. In a great turn of fortune, being elected meant that I'd be in the same role for the rest of my time as a cadet. Applying for assignments and trying to make rank no longer applied to me. It was like being appointed to the Supreme Court. My job was to enforce the Academy's code that, "We will not lie, cheat, or steal; nor tolerate among us anyone who does." My assignment consisted of preparing and conducting Honor Boards without any attachment to my squadron, so I went about my business, focused on my coursework, and never looked back. I became a ghost; absent from formations and training activities. Aspiring to the Air Force's corps values of *integrity first, service before self, and excellence in all we do* became my identity. I'd reached a point when I realized being a warrior isn't just about combat; it's about being a person who's not afraid to make the right choice—even if it comes at your sacrifice. That's the realization it took to graduate.

○ ○ ○

Once we were commissioned as officers and started our service on active duty, we were assigned to specific career fields. While the first choice for many of my peers was to go to pilot training, I came to the decision that I'd flown enough in my life as a traveler and a cadet in high school with a pilot's license in Civil Air Patrol that sitting in a confined space for long periods of time wasn't something I was interested in doing long-term. In my mind, I was a person capable of rapidly learning and adapting to situations in the field, so there was an aspect of working in military intelligence beyond the way popular media glamorizes agents that influenced my decision.

After I received my Top Secret security clearance, Intelligence training began in the barren landscape of West Texas at Goodfellow Air Force Base in San Angelo. The content of the training is classified, but I can summarize that the days consisted of checking into a highly restricted Sensitive Compartmented Information Facility without windows for long hours followed by drinking in dive bars because there was nothing else to do in town. For reasons I'll later explain, I fell into a deep depression and realized that I'd made one of the worst decisions of my life. My career would be sentenced to doing analysis essentially chained to a computer building briefings for decision makers. The further I advanced in the training, the more resistant I grew to the type of work we'd be doing. This attitude led to several counseling sessions about my negative attitude and poor performance on subjects they knew I'd already mastered as an Air Force Academy graduate. I saw two ways out: either purposefully fail or insist on being reassigned.

Unfortunately, a threat that loomed over my thinking was that we'd been told that failure to graduate would result in losing our commission and having to repay the cost of our education. Remember the $250,000 number that caught my attention in high school? Taking on that sort of debt would've put me into crippling bankruptcy, and my preference was to stay in the military, so I wrote a letter requesting reassignment. My peers and the command staff were mystified why someone who'd worked so hard to be entrusted with such a specialized role in the military would throw it all away, but I had my reasons. In response, the Air Force decided to reassign me to a career field that was generally viewed as the job no one wanted to do: Services.

The Services career field is an amalgamation of a number of different support programs for soldiers and their dependents. Everything from food, fitness, and lodging operations to mortuary arrangements and career transitioning falls under its umbrella. I can recall being told *How the mighty have fallen!* when I was reassigned because the work is generally considered menial and far less glamorous than being a fighter pilot or pararescue operator, but I didn't mind. No longer shackled to a computer in a secure facility, I was freed to help manage dozens of different projects across base operations that kept my days varied. It also helped that my next duty station moved me from Texas to Edwards Air Force Base located in the barren desert of southern California.

After attending a brief few weeks of training in Ohio at Wright-Patterson Air Force Base, I reported for duty with the 412th Mission Support Group attached to the Air Force Flight Test Center made famous by pilots like Chuck Yeager when he broke the sound barrier in 1947. Due to classified flight testing requirements and contingency operations like serving as a landing base for space shuttles, Edwards encompasses

470 square miles of restricted airspace surrounded by guarded fencing. From the main entrance gate to the actual base, it's roughly a 25-minute drive. Thankfully, my role required me to live on station in officers quarters, so I avoided the long daily commute that the majority of soldiers had to make.

My supervisor was a suit and tie type of civilian responsible for Services operations at the squadron level. Mr. Wilson had lived around the world as a government employee and we struck up an immediate rapport over traveling and the humanities. Each military station has a club with a bar and restaurant run by Services where people can go for lunch or dinner, so he told me to meet there after work for drinks to get to know the employees as well as meet his supervisor and my commander, a towering 6'6" cowboy from New Mexico who had made a career of working in fuels. His physical appearance was intimidating, but he had a great sense of humor and a booming laugh. Colonel Wooley's first words to me were, "Do you drink bourbon, LT?" My reply should be obvious and he declared, "I like you, LT. You're going to be my new bird dog." Several pours of bourbon later, he decided I wouldn't be working at the squadron level; I'd be replacing a seasoned captain (two ranks above me) as Colonel Wooley's new Executive Officer.

Regardless of your experience, the rank of Lieutenant is a signal of ignorance, so executing a Colonel's orders by working with senior enlisted soldiers who roll their eyes at you and ranking officers who ignore you entirely makes what seems like the easiest of tasks require dogged tenacity. Once again, I needed to prove myself, so I set out to gain the respect of the leaders on station by taking on the additional role of being the Officer in Charge of the base Honor Guard responsible for military ceremonies across southern California. Every day presented different challenges and required me to venture out to meet people or do something physical. While I answered a lot of phone calls and served as watchdog for Colonel Wooley with a desk that guarded his office; I was the person he trusted to go out and be his eyes in the field. It meant a lot to me and it's the sort of work that made me proud to be in the military. I gradually realized that I wasn't meant for being in the air for hours or targeting enemies from a Top Secret facility. In a way, I wanted to be the sort of soldier who took care of everyone in the unit like those who supported me growing up.

The memories that stand out the most from my assignment to Edwards include a search and recovery mission to collect the remains of an F-15 that crashed in a remote part of the desert, watching the space shuttle land after being diverted from Florida, and my final detail for the Honor Guard: escorting our base commander's widow to Arlington National Ceremony. I'd worked for Colonel Gallagher on a number of different projects and grew to admire his leadership. The day before he passed away, I'd noticed that he was looking unusually pale, but I didn't say anything. The following morning, he had a massive heart attack in his car after working out at the gym. His wife Robyn was one of my favorite people to socialize with at the club whenever we hosted events, so my heart broke for her loss. Colonel Woolley knew we were friends and gave me orders to support her in any way she needed, so I assisted with funeral arrangements, made all the travel plans, and was by her side at Arlington to hold her hand when the volleys for his 21-gun salute were fired followed by the playing of "Taps."

When we returned, I was faced with a major decision: extend my commission as an officer for another four years or submit my paperwork for separation so I could start graduate school. Staying in the military offered a sense of familiarity and security because I'd known it my whole life, while separating represented an opportunity to start a new chapter in my life and continue to develop my mind. It was a red-or-blue-pill choice like in *The Matrix*. Colonel Woolley called me into his office for a conversation about the decision and his advice surprised me. He recommended that I pursue a doctorate and become an educator, so I promised him that I would become a professor and submitted my paperwork for separation. A few weeks later, my request was approved with a scheduled date of June 11–the same day I was commissioned from the Air Force Academy. That day, I was promoted to the rank of Captain and assigned to the inactive reserve. It was time to learn how to be more than a warrior.

The Scholar
(The Manager)

There's a common misconception that people who pursue a path of scholarship and become academic professionals are "Straight-A" students. This couldn't be further from the truth in my case. Knowledge is specific to a subject; and mastery of a given field doesn't cross apply to others. You can be a highly intelligent person and still fail to comprehend how to operate a forklift. Everyone learns at different rates and levels of interest. For example, I've always been poor at the hard sciences like engineering, physics, and chemistry–courses I actually failed in college. However, subjects related to the humanities, communication, and writing are strengths that carried me through an incredibly difficult curriculum at the Air Force Academy followed by multiple graduate degrees including a doctorate.

The first time I heard of someone earning a doctoral degree was when my middle school principal was recognized over the daily announcements. He was a tall African-American gentleman with a backstory of growing up in rural Texas sleeping on the floor of a one-bedroom home and lifting cinder blocks as weights. I only met him once when I was sent to his office, and of course it was for mouthing off to a teacher. I'd just learned the term "double-chin" and couldn't help but announce in class that our portly drama teacher's exemplary jowls could be featured in an encyclopedia. The principal was less than amused and assigned me to detention to think about why my comment was hurtful. His intimidating presence was enough to make sure I never had to go to his office again, and in a way I began to associate higher education with authority.

While my parents ended up going to college later in their lives and both of my aunts have advanced degrees, I really didn't have an understanding of higher education as a system with an increasingly challenging curriculum. My concept of college was largely shaped by watching sports until I started high school. I can recall the only assistance from our guidance counselor I ever received was being handed a book of over a thousand pages listing every college in the United States that proved less than helpful. Once I began seeing older students go to schools I only knew about by watching television, the idea of doing the same started to motivate my focus on academics. Grades began to mean more to me and introduced a new anxiety of not getting accepted by a "good" college. I knew that the standards for getting into a service academy were extremely difficult to reach, and I've never been one to give up on my goals, so I put a lot of pressure on my academic performance.

My biggest challenge was all of my other interests that took time away from completing assignments that should have taken priority. I was always playing sports, volunteering for JROTC, going to leadership conferences, or generally doing any extra curricular activities that I found more engaging than learning Chemistry or Physics. I was the type of student who earned good grades without a large amount of effort, but I was never the most focused person in a class. My high school in Germany was operated by the Department of Defense Dependent Schools and I can attest that our teachers were generally more experienced and qualified than the public systems I'd been enrolled in over the years. They offered Honors, Advanced Placement (AP), and Computer-Aided Design courses that prepared me well for success in college.

By the spring semester of my senior year, all of my classes had a college-level curriculum or were free for work study because I already had enough credits to graduate, so I served as an assistant for my two favorite teachers: Ms. Judy Flacke for AP History and Mr. John Robert for AP Literature. I'd always been a voracious reader of nonfiction as well as prose, so in looking ahead to college I began to consider either of their subjects as my future major. Letters of acceptance started arriving in the mail from state universities, with my safety school being the University of Michigan on an Army ROTC scholarship, but I was standing by for decisions from the service academies. After being waitlisted at West Point and receiving the Falcon scholarship for the Air Force Academy, I turned to advice from Mr. Robert. Rather than handing me a book or giving vague suggestions, he was the only person who gave me a specific recommendation to attend the school that would provide the best possible education: take the opportunity offered by the Air Force Academy. It's a decision that I've never regretted from an academic perspective.

○ ○ ○

Most people think that service academies prioritize military training before academics, but it's quite the opposite. Their faculties represent some of the greatest minds in the military as well as distinguished civilian educators. The curriculum stresses the value of core competencies, so every cadet takes a set sequence of courses from every academic department and graduates with a Bachelor of Science degree without an option for a Bachelor of Arts. In turn, whether I chose to major in English or History, I'd still have to pass courses like Electromagnetic Physics, Thermodynamics, and Astronautical Engineering. The next four years would prove more difficult than any of the graduate courses I'd take later in life. My saving grace was my training and ability as a writer—a skill that was valued across the curriculum.

When faced with what subject to major in, the decision came down to either History or English. The former didn't allow much room for creativity and the latter's department sponsored the Speech and Debate team, so I declared English in my first semester and never doubted the decision. There were only eight cadets from my class that made the same choice, so we got to know each other well since we all basically took the same courses together for the next four years. The first class that made a significant impact on my perspective was Introduction to Critical Methods taught by a brilliant civilian instructor named Dr. Richard Lemp who always wore a suit and tie to class. It was the first time I'd been exposed to critiques of media from the lens of race, gender, authorship, and historical context that became highly influential in my studies. I quickly realized that criticism could be cross-applied far beyond literature and began viewing media in a new way–particularly cinema.

Growing up in the era of VHS tapes, watching movies exposed me to a wide spectrum of stories at an early age that provided me with a sense of empathy for people in different situations from my own. I loved international films, documentaries, and independent movies from the start. My appreciation for the other elements of filmmaking would come later, but how screenplays were constructed was fascinating to me as a writer. I became so fascinated that during the summer between my year in New Mexico and starting at the Academy, I wrote my first feature-length screenplay. The process began with blindly placing my finger on a map, a town called Blythe between the border of Arizona and California, and creating a story about what it would be like to live there and how someone might feel if they decided to leave–a subconscious theme that drove a lot of my creative writing projects in college.

After telling my advisor about my interest in screenwriting, he introduced me to another professor in the English department who specialized in Film Criticism. From our first conversation, I knew that the Professor was going to be an influential figure in my education. The Professor read my screenplay and provided copious notes in his eloquent style of cursive. My first course from him was a survey of Science Fiction that I loved because it extended the critical approaches from Dr. Lemp's analysis in literature to genre filmmaking. The class provided me with a vocabulary to intellectually discuss cinema that paved the way for earning my first graduate degree in Film and Media Studies.

After the course, I began taking independent study projects with the Professor and he would hand me stacks of VHS tapes of obscure films that I'd visually devour. He gave me the foundation for understanding the value of direction, editing, sound, cinematography, and performance play in creating films that are worthy of studying. We'd meet in his office every other week and have an academic conversation in a manner similar to oral exams in the British school system. He was the sort of person with an encyclopedic memory for everything from composer names to the year's movies were produced, so I drew inspiration from his example and made it a goal to reach a similar command of the medium. Over the better part of three years, before he transferred to teach at the Naval Academy, I studied over 500 films with his guidance, published several essays in journals, wrote two more feature-length screenplays, served as a writer and director for the Academy's television channel, and was selected as the first person from a service academy to attend the Telluride Film Festival's student program.

○ ○ ○

I was also fortunate to have two other instructors in the English department, Professor Rachel Woodward and Major Doug Cunningham, who coached our Speech and Debate team. In my freshman year, I competed in Parliamentary Debate, Impromptu and Extemporaneous Speaking as well as Dramatic Interpretation. I was proud of winning one of the largest tournaments in the country in debate with my partner, Justin Hickey, and our team ultimately winning Overall Season Sweepstakes in the nation due to the leadership of our seniors. However, my first season taught me that my strength was much more in preparation rather than an ability to quickly develop a response under time pressure, so I transitioned to focusing specifically on speech events.

I didn't compete in high school, but I quickly learned that the world of collegiate speech (or Individual Events) is a subculture occupied by incredibly driven students, rigorous performance expectations, extremely technical judging, and an infuriating number of unwritten conventions that are often dictated by programs with budgets that can afford to perennially recruit championship talent. The structure of tournaments consists of two or three preliminary rounds where students are randomly assigned to groups of six where a judge assigns ranks per contestant. For example, the "best" performance in a system rife with subjectivity earns a rank of 1 and the worst is assigned a rank of 5. The ranks from preliminary rounds are tabulated and then the top students advance to additional rounds that conclude with Finals. The competition schedule spans the entire school year and is grueling for everyone involved. Tournaments generally run from 8am-6pm for both days of the weekend and there's rarely a lunch break. Moreover, the amount of travel time involves being on the road every other weekend for long hours cramped in a 15-passenger van trying to memorize speeches and complete homework.

Combined, working on projects for my major as well as competing in speech and debate diverted the majority of my time from focusing on the core courses needed to graduate—just like I'd done in high school. As a freshman, I hobbled my way through Chemistry, Biology, and Computer Science; but failed Physics. In turn, I had to go on Academic Probation and wasn't allowed to travel to the National Speech Tournament I qualified for after winning competitions over the course of the season. I can still recall everyone's disappointment; especially the seniors who led the team.

Letting them down was motivation enough not to fail another class, so I retook Physics over the summer and doubled my academic efforts in my sophomore year. If it wasn't a Liberal Arts subject where I could rely on writing and come up with creative solutions to assignments, I made sure I went to office hours with my professors and sought tutoring from my peers. While I can't say that I've retained much of the principles covered in classes like Calculus or Electrical Engineering, one of the most important lessons I learned from taking the required core curriculum was realizing that it's possible to pass a course, or challenge, in almost any subject as long as you invest the necessary time and accept assistance when you need help.

Of all of the subjects I studied in college, competing in speech and debate provided the most valuable learning experience because the activity is composed of students and coaches from all walks of life completely disconnected from the military. Debate taught me how to defend perspectives other than my own on issues, and speech taught me how to authentically listen to and consider their arguments. Together with the documentaries and international films I was studying, the value of the activity was far beyond building skills as a competitor; it was a learning laboratory for building empathy. In Debate events, we'd regularly have to take positions such as advocating (in uniform) for peace against barefooted students from Liberal Arts colleges like Berkeley calling for nuclear holocaust. Conversely, speech events often served as a platform for competitors to share their personal experiences since topics were always of the students own selection.

At the start of my competitive career the material I chose to perform was often adapted from the screenplays of some of my favorite films like *Network*, *Monty Python's Meaning of Life*, and *Swimming with Sharks* without much of a rationale for using the material. However, as I listened to my peers make arguments that I'd never heard of about identity politics such as feminism, racism, and homophobia, I became inspired to explore issues that I'd personally struggled with such as interracial dating, accidental military fatalities, and escapism from trauma. The process of researching, taking a position, and performing my own interpretation of the literature on the subjects proved incredibly therapeutic and shifted the focus of my academic studies toward more applied than theoretical research.

By the time I was a senior, I'd grown into a role where I was student coaching our novice members and individually advanced to National Semifinals for the first time in over a decade for our team. I also published several creative writing stories and academic papers on media studies that positioned me to earn a rare slot to go directly to graduate school and return to the Academy to teach. While that possibility didn't end up materializing for me because I finished second in my major to another student, I knew that I wanted to pursue an advanced degree in the future, but it would have to wait until I completed my military service.

○ ○ ○

Years later, when I submitted my separation paperwork from the Air Force, I enrolled in a Masters program for Film and Media Studies at Arizona State University. Tempe had always been my favorite location from the many speech and debate competitions we'd gone to at ASU for when I was an undergraduate, so I was excited to continue my studies, take on a coaching role, and pursue a career in education. Since Academy graduates who were selected to return to teach were expected to complete their degrees in a year, even though Masters level coursework usually takes two or more, I set the ambitious goal of finishing mine in the same amount of time.

In turn, I immediately began taking summer courses and doubled my course load for the next two semesters, so I could defend my thesis the following July. My advisor was skeptical, but after I took one of his courses he realized that my skillset, experience, and determination were far beyond the average student in the program. I recall him asking where I learned to write and raising his eyebrows when I attributed my training in the humanities to the Air Force Academy. Similarly, my peers fixated on my being a veteran and somehow assumed that was synonymous with being uneducated, so I took it as a challenge to change their perception of soldiers.

I also started working with undergraduate students by coaching on the Speech and Debate team at ASU. There were about 20 members on the team with five graduate student coaches who met nearly every afternoon in our squad room to practice. In contrast to my team at the Academy, ASU had won scores of National Championships and was consistently ranked in the Top 10 programs in the country, so it was an exciting opportunity to work with such talented competitors and alumni. The downside was that coaching required driving a passenger van to transport students every other weekend for tournaments where the entire days were spent judging. Combined with my coursework, my schedule was as exhausting as working two fulltime jobs, but I enjoyed being back in an academic environment that was mentally stimulating and particularly rewarding to see the students on the team achieve their goals.

Unfortunately, when the economy took a sudden downturn in 2008 our team's budget was one of the first programs to be cancelled by the Communication department. Allocated funds needed to be exhausted by the end of the season, so the students were devastated and left with the daunting challenge of trying to raise funds by themselves. Moreover, it was announced that our graduate student coaches would lose their scholarships at the conclusion of the school year, so the team was left with turning to alumni and volunteers like myself to take them to tournaments.

The news cast a pall over everyone and as the season advanced the feelings grew even more intense as the students began the process of mourning for the impending loss of their place in the community. As a coaching staff, we went so far as to dress in black for the final day of the National Championships like we were attending a funeral. One of our students on the team, Andy Stone, even gave a farewell speech that spoke for us all in the final round of the tournament structured in the Kubler-Ross model known as the Five Stages of Grief: Denial, Anger, Bargaining, Depression, and Acceptance. At the awards ceremony, it was announced that the team had finished 7th in the nation and we received a standing ovation that still overwhelms me as our peers gave us a collective "goodbye."

After the season ended, I spent the summer finishing my graduate degree in Film and Media Studies by writing, producing, and directing a short film set in the art gallery district of Old Town Scottsdale. Given the option of writing a thesis or doing an applied project, I was energized by returning to screenwriting and working behind the camera on creative projects like I did at the Air Force Academy. I'd written a feature-length screenplay for one of my graduate courses called *Creative Differences* that was based on my husband's relationship co-owning an art gallery with his business partner, but we unfortunately didn't have the resources to make a feature film, so in order to satisfy the requirements for my degree, I crafted a backstory about two of the characters that worked as a short film titled *On the Third Date* that we were able to make on a shoestring budget. The project took months of pre-production storyboarding and planning the logistics for a three-day shoot followed by weeks of editing in post-production before premiering the film for my graduation defense. The screening only lasted 14 minutes in a small auditorium on campus, but it was gratifying to have my peers in the program along with students from the Speech and Debate team come to support me.

○ ○ ○

After I graduated in the summer, I applied for instructor roles at a number of local community colleges and was hired to teach Introduction to Composition at Phoenix College, Introduction to Film History at Scottsdale Community College, and the Communication Department at ASU gave me several sections of Public Speaking as a source of income to help cover for all of my work volunteering to coach the team. In turn, teaching six classes basically replaced taking an overload of graduate courses in my schedule—all while coaching most afternoons and spending weekends judging at tournaments. The part of me that always needs to raise the difficulty level on my goals was in high gear and I put a lot of pressure on myself to be the sort of educator like John Robert and the Professor who inspired me to pursue a career in higher education.

It took me a while to adapt to being in the front of the classroom. Not from a sense of nervousness, but because the majority of students really weren't interested in the material or engaged in discussions. The standards that were expected of me in college were completely different from the culture of partying at a large state university. My emphasis on organization, discipline, and following instructions came across too seriously and *militant* in my evaluations. Academia was a completely different environment than the military. Admittedly, I was too rigid as an instructor and can see how the intensity of my schedule translated into my tone being stressful. Once I acknowledged the feedback and gradually adjusted my standards to be more reasonable, I became more comfortable and approachable as a professor. A common piece of advice for educators is that you can teach the same course every year, or you can make your course better every year. I've always focused on the latter and this approach to evaluating performance, and curriculum became a major influence on my scholarly research.

Another professional lesson I quickly learned is that having multiple part-time jobs will never offer the security of having a full-time career. Teaching six courses with roughly

30 students in each across three campuses while coaching was far from sustainable because my paychecks cobbled together were barely $40,000 before taxes. I needed a salaried role, but it was next to impossible to find a position in Film and Media Studies, so my husband recommended I go back to school for another graduate degree. Since there were more opportunities in Communication departments, and I already had the experience of teaching Public Speaking as well as coaching speech and debate, I grudgingly agreed to enroll in night courses at ASU's West campus rather than take classes from my peers on the Tempe campus. The commute took 45 minutes each way and the entire experience was sponsored by coffee. My days turned into teaching in the morning, coaching in the afternoon, and going to classes in the evening.

If I was going to burn the candle at both ends again, I decided that my goal would be to complete my Masters in Communication Studies in a year as well. This time, I had two advantages that made the challenge less daunting than when I transitioned out of the military: my familiarity with the structure and content of graduate courses as well as professional experience teaching Communication. It also helped before starting the program that I already had a direction for my thesis as part of my time spent evaluating courses; particularly those offered virtually. A prominent part of online education requires students to participate in discussion boards where they respond to prompts related to the coursework and then "interact" with other students by replying to a minimum number of posts. From my own experience, however, online discussions rarely facilitate engagement between students as well as instructors like they do in a physical classroom, so I grew curious about how to improve interaction in such assignments.

As I advanced through my coursework, I read through stacks of education journals for reference articles and leveraged all of the discussion-board materials in the classes I took to help develop a study for my thesis designed to measure student engagement in forums. While I was working on my thesis, I began taking elective courses in the School of Education related to Instructional Design and Technology–specific branches of research that center on the study of learning theories and the development of contemporary teaching practices. After teaching and coaching for four years, I'd gained a lot of practical knowledge and personal experience that allowed me to take what I was learning and directly apply the concepts to my own classes. The design of curriculum and how courses are constructed for online and hybrid delivery quickly became the focus of my research and drove my decision to pursue a Ph.D. in Educational Technology.

The first time I can recall having an interest in curriculum design was when I took a 400-level seminar at the Air Force Academy on Modern American Literature taught by the most senior member of the English

Department, Dr. Fred Kiley. While I admired his teaching style, my main critique of the course was that virtually all of the reading selections were written by white men, so when it came time to compose the final paper for the class I decided to deviate from the prompt and completely redesign his syllabus–long before Diversity, Equity, and Inclusion policies became popular–to feature more diverse authors like James Baldwin and Harper Lee. As a senior, I worried that Dr. Kiley might fail me for not following the instructions, but he ended up sharing it with the entire class and faculty as one of his favorite submissions for a final project. That moment foreshadowed how my path would eventually lead to becoming a professor and research scientist.

○ ○ ○

A decade later, I successfully defended my doctoral dissertation in the fall semester of 2014 titled, *Learning to Speak in the Digital Age: An Examination of Instructional Conditions for Teaching Public Speaking Online*. Since the credits for my second Master's degree counted as electives toward my doctorate, I was able to complete the program in half of what normally takes the average student five years–all while teaching, coaching, and traveling. By this point, my mind and body had become conditioned to constantly staying *busy* and productive, so it only made sense at the time to doggedly push forward. I knew that I'd never earn a salaried tenure-track role at a university unless I completed a terminal degree like a Ph.D. and that professional insecurity fueled my determination.

Based on my experience coaching and teaching Public Speaking, I chose to research approaches to delivering content for the course in different modalities. I was particularly curious about how students would perform when various conditions like taking the class online, so I devised an experiment to statistically measure performance using a theory developed by one of our faculty members at ASU named Dr. Micki Chi that's referred to as the ICAP (Interactive, Constructive, Active, and Passive) framework. Essentially, the theory categorizes student engagement into four levels, hypothesizing that higher levels of engagement lead to deeper learning: Interactive engagement, Constructive activities, then Active listening, and finally Passive observation.

Completing my doctorate triggered a number of significant life changes in a short period. Earning a terminal degree allowed me to achieve my professional goal of landing a job with long-term security by accepting a salaried role teaching for the University of Maryland's Global Campus. For the next two years, I taught communication and film history courses in Germany, Spain, and England. Without taking graduate courses in the evening and driving students to tournaments, my schedule was suddenly open to do something other than work, so my husband and I took the opportunity to travel as much as we could throughout Europe. Our weekends were spent on trains exploring cities like Berlin and Amsterdam, relaxing on the beaches of the Costa del Sol in Spain, and flying to the Arctic Circle to see the Northern Lights. It was a point in my marriage when we'd emerged on the other side of a long period of being overworked and were finally able to enjoy our time together.

Moreover, I connected with teaching soldiers and their dependents far more than I had at a large state university. Plus my workload was dramatically less than teaching six sections of courses across multiple locations, so my tone and comfort in the classroom started to reflect in my evaluations. Somehow I was more *intense* with civilian students, but *chill* with soldiers in the military. My significant improvement as an instructor came through deeply studying the craft of teaching in my graduate work and the sheer volume of repetitions I'd accumulated being in front of a classroom. As a result, much to my surprise, I received a Teaching Recognition Award at the end of my first year abroad. I was at the height of my professional abilities and the part of me that had always been in top gear applying pressure to myself to manage everything eventually started to relax.

○ ○ ○

Returning to the United States, I accepted a part-time role teaching Film History at ASU again to help bridge the gap in my loss of salary from the University of Maryland. Time spent traveling abroad turned into mornings applying for jobs and self-isolation trying to figure out how to recover from the sacrifice. Watching my husband revel in his impending retirement while I was desperately trying to find gainful employment drove a wedge of resentment between us. I began to regret leaving my job abroad and the thought kept playing in my mind like a depressing song on repeat. I needed to find a new tune in a key other than teaching, so in the events of *A Year in Waiting* when I was offered a job from a friend to be a waiter at one of the best restaurants in the world it sounded like a chance worth taking. I was beginning to question whether the part of me that had built my identity around being a professor had made the right choice and decided it was time to face that insecurity in order to evolve. *If I wasn't going to be a teacher anymore, then what was I going to be?*

The Queer
(The Exile)

I didn't come out as gay until I was in my mid-20s and left the military. It wasn't permissible to be homosexual in the community I grew up in, so the only examples of gay men I saw were in the media where they were generally portrayed as either funny or abhorrent–always *different* from the way average Americans are represented. Keep in mind that this was before the onset of the internet gave people access to the collective knowledge of humanity. We didn't have *Ru Paul's Drag Race* on a streaming service, we had Paul Lynde in *Hollywood Squares* on an antenna receiver. Being gay was something to conceal in order to avoid shame or persecution. In turn, I became conditioned never to give the perception of having any mannerisms, speech patterns, or appearance associated with being a *queer*.

In the year I started middle school and the onset of puberty began, we moved from the inland desert of southern California to the rolling plains of western Texas. Until that point, I can't recall anyone accusing me of being gay, but my voice took longer to deepen than my peers and bullies taught me a new word: faggot. Replying with wordplay that you're not a collection of sticks doesn't really work on anyone without a vocabulary, so you learn to find other means of deflecting negative attention. For me, dealing with antagonists pragmatically boiled down to a strategy of either proving my value through athletics or helping kids with their homework. The latter worked until I got caught by the librarian taking tests for other students. I was like a bar regular at the library and I can still recall the look of disappointment the stout German librarian gave me when she realized I was taking tests for other students. It's still a moment of shame I'll never forget. As a result, I earned an on-campus suspension for a week, which meant that I was put in the grade school version of solitary confinement seated in an empty room at a cubicle to read and do my homework. When I returned to class shy of being a hardened criminal, I was a month ahead of the other students on homework and earned the respect of the gang members I was taking tests for by not snitching. It was the best punishment I've ever received.

After that point, I was left alone by the tougher kids, but a new anxiety set in when we started Physical Education classes and were forced to change in front of each other in the locker room–even the coaches. I never recall being distracted by any of my peers getting undressed, but I subconsciously began to gawk at one of the football coaches in his 40s with graying ginger hair and a burly chest who would strip down to a bleach-white jock strap before squeezing into the tight gym shorts of the era and a white polo. It was a visual magnetism to an aesthetic that I didn't understand at the time but that would later define my sexual type.

At the start of seventh grade, we were separated by gender for a Sexual Education class, and I remember very little of the course other than daydreaming about the instructor. By this time I'd seen magazines and VHS tapes that featured soft pornography, but there was never any gay content that I'd seen or the class taught. Sex was defined for us as intercourse between a man and woman, so it never occurred to me that the reason my gaze kept fixating on mature men as sources of attraction was because they looked like the ones I'd seen featured in magazines like *GQ* and *Esquire*. Flirting with girls was a part of fitting in, and some boys my age were already having sex, so showing a shared interest was part of beginning to mask my personal identity that lasted through high school and college.

By the time we moved to Germany in 1996, my voice had lowered and I learned how to pass as a straight boy. Some girls even began to show an interest in me, but it took me years to muster the courage to kiss one of my best friends when we went to the Prom together. I didn't even date women or have any sexual fumblings until I started college. My gaze kept fixating on men and the thought began to occur to me that the kids in Texas knew who I was long before I'd admit it to myself. Maybe I really was queer, but that was a conversation I'd bury deep in my subconscious in order to keep my identity safe while I served in the military.

○ ○ ○

During the time I spent in the Air Force as a cadet and an officer, there was a policy called "Don't Ask, Don't Tell" that prohibited even speaking about one's own homosexuality under the threat of being dishonorably discharged from the service. The anxiety of anyone finding out you were gay was terrifying and created a culture of willful ignorance within the military that turned its back on the very people fighting side-by-side with their straight counterparts for freedom. Some service members would go so far as to test their peers to prove their sexuality. For example, one of my classmates at New Mexico Military Institute who ended up going to the Army's service academy at West Point was baited with instant messages from someone posing as another gay student at a neighboring college trying to arrange a hook-up. My friend agreed to meet, but when he arrived the Military Police were waiting to arrest him. There was no recourse and after he was kicked out we completely lost touch because I was too scared to be associated with the situation. The stakes felt like playing poker with everything you own on the line.

During my second year at the Air Force Academy, I was tested in the exact same way. One afternoon I received a random message from someone portraying themselves as a visiting cadet from West Point who heard I was gay and wanted to meet. Since I knew my response would be recorded, I immediately denied the rumor, blocked their account, and actually considered destroying the laptop. I couldn't figure out why whoever was behind the account chose to approach me and paranoia set in as my mind churned over trying to identify whatever mistake I'd made to conceal the identity that was becoming increasingly difficult to hide as my thoughts about men gradually became more sexual.

One of my greatest frustrations growing up was an inability to develop friendships with adults; especially when it became unprofessional to fraternize with instructors. A prime example was my relationship with the Professor. He had a lean build, Alabaster skin, combed over hair, and circular lenses in his glasses–far from the stocky football coach type, but I immediately fell for the contours of his face. I reported to his office to have my transcript evaluated for whether I qualified to validate and skip Introduction to Composition. He squinted his blue eyes at the paper and an amused look came across his face as he scoffed at the *A-* I'd earned at NMMI and said, "By the skin of your teeth, Butler." He had a manner about him that was unlike any of the other instructors and a smile crossed my face as I said, "Thank you, sir," saluted smartly, and left wondering when I'd get a chance to talk to him again.

At my first speech and debate tournament, the Professor served as a judge and I was excited to speak to him between rounds of competition. It was the first time I saw him in civilian clothes wearing a mustard-colored suit with a white button-up shirt–far from the appearance of a typical military officer. The Professor was the sort of creative intellectual I aspired to be, and I quickly grew infatuated with wanting to get to know him better. There was something about the way he carried himself that was *different* in a familiar way. This was a person who would never say it aloud, but crossed his legs, spoke in code, and used mannerisms that were gay to anyone paying attention. I can recall another instructor making fun of the way the Professor *sashayed* into faculty meetings, but I saw the way he carried himself as courageous. He was the first person I'd met who was likely gay.

Over the next three years his mentorship gradually grew into a friendship. I took a course with him that led to two independent studies where we'd regularly meet in his office. He started giving me movies to watch that served as a form of communication without us explicitly talking about being queer. The gay themes in some of the films began to feel like a metacommentary on our own situation and we eventually started going to the independent theater together on the weekends. By this time, I'd developed an obsession with him that I couldn't shake, and I can only imagine how difficult it was for him to navigate how to maintain a professional relationship between us without risking our being discharged despite never being intimate with each other. One afternoon while driving to the theater I finally gathered up the courage to ask him about what I should do about being gay, but he immediately told me that was a conversation that we couldn't have and endangered us both, so I never broached the subject again. I'd have to settle for the advice he gave me through the lessons in the movies we watched.

Unfortunately, someone in the English Department eventually took notice and reported us for having an unprofessional relationship. The terror of the instant message baiting all came flooding back, but this time a person I'd grown to deeply care for was having his career threatened, so the stakes were twice as high. As part of the investigation, we weren't allowed to interact with each other for months and I fell into a deep depression. Seeing the Professor always brought a smile to my face and spending time with him had become a rare source of happiness during my time as a cadet. I kept every movie ticket we ever went to in a sentimental keepsake box at the back of my dresser door like a secret, and was admittedly guilty of making unprofessional advances to meet with the Professor off campus, so I blamed myself for the feelings I struggled to control. Not being able to communicate frustrated me to no end, and I couldn't stop thinking about how likely it was that we wouldn't be able to see each other again, so a part of me began to self-sabotage our friendship by expecting him to find a way to reach out to me.

Once the investigation ended, there was no evidence that was enough to punish us, but the warning was clear that we needed to keep our distance. Whether it was a coincidence or not, the Professor received a new assignment and moved over the summer to the East coast. I felt like I was being abandoned and the protector in me lashed out. The last film we saw together was *Lost in Translation*, which is a quiet story about Bob and Charlotte who make an unexpected connection while traveling that they can't act on. There's an age gap between the two and the sexual tension between them reflected the sort of relationship the Professor and I shared. At the movie's conclusion, the two embrace as they have to part ways and Bob whispers a message to Charlotte that's never explained. As the credits started to roll, my eyes welled with tears and I turned to the Professor who was trying to restrain the same feeling. I wanted my first kiss with a man to be at that moment, but we found ourselves in the same situation as Bob and Charlotte. I still wish he would've whispered something in my ear to reassure me that we'd see each other again, but after the stress of the investigation the last time we spoke I showed up at his home with my box of movie tickets and gave it to him as a symbol of us parting ways. It's an act of immaturity that I still regret, but felt I needed to do at the time in order to move forward after he left. Like many fans of *Lost in Translation*, I keep hoping that they'll make a sequel and there's more of a happy ending to their story, but perhaps there's more truth in relationships that end tragically.

○ ○ ○

My first kiss with a man led to a marriage that would last 15 years. I first met my future husband at a conference in Chicago for Communication scholars when I was serving as the student representative for the National Speech

Tournament in my final year at the Air Force Academy. It was the first time I'd been to an academic conference and I loved being immersed in conversations with the ranks of professors I wanted to join. Evenings were spent at mixers with scholars from all over the world and that's where I was introduced to a man with all of the features and style of the Professor, but void of any ties to the military. Our eyes caught each other from across the room and I asked a friend to introduce us despite having no idea what I was doing trying to flirt with someone 25 years my senior. All I knew was that this was a person I felt magnetized to and after only a few minutes of conversation made me start thinking of what it would be like for us to spend more time together.

Months later, we got our chance during Spring Break when I drove to Arizona with friends and split the week between Phoenix and Las Vegas. It was a time when text messaging was starting to be popular prior to the advent of smart phones, so we had been communicating by tapping buttons multiple times on our Nokia phones just to type a character. That's how motivated you needed to be. While tedious, texting allowed us to get to know each other more and correspond without having a conversation that someone might overhear. I knew that joining my friends on their trip would allow me some time to meet my future husband in person again, so the anticipation was building for what might happen. We hadn't brought up anything sexual between us, but there was a mutual interest that excited us both.

Once we arrived in Arizona, I immediately reached out to him, and we arranged to meet for dinner with two of our mutual friends at a gay-owned restaurant called *Hamburger Mary's.* This was the first time I'd been anywhere associated with being queer, so there was some anxiety that the military would somehow find out and I wouldn't graduate, but my heart told me to be brave and start unlearning everything I'd been taught about the evils of homosexuality. Having dinner with men who were out of the closet made me feel like I'd finally found my true community. Listening to their stories, learning their vocabulary, and being in a space where that was safe showed me what my life might be like if I left the military.

The following afternoon, my future husband invited the three of us to his home for lunch in the neighborhood of Ahwatukee on the edge of the South Mountain Preserve. His two-story home in the suburbs backed up to an arroyo filled with cactus and Palo Verde trees that served as a relaxing backdrop dining outside by the pool. He gave me a tour of the upstairs rooms and flirted by touching my shoulder and sticking his tongue out like a turtle when he teased me verbally–the sort of affection that I'd fantasized about for years. When it came time for me to leave I finally got my chance to show him I was just as interested. He walked me to the door where we had a moment of privacy and I kissed him with every ounce of passion I'd been bottling inside myself. He lingered in the doorway with a look of glee on his face as I waved goodbye; both of us knowing this was only the beginning.

After graduating from the Air Force Academy, cadets are given 60 days of leave to visit their families and take vacation prior to reporting for their first duty assignment. While the majority of my friends went on adventures or trips abroad, my only plans were to drive to Arizona and be with my future husband. We'd been corresponding since Spring Break, and the kiss we shared lived in my mind rent-free for months. I drove so fast from Colorado Springs to Phoenix that the regulator for limiting my speed kicked in around 115 mph–thankfully without being pulled over or getting in an accident. I drove directly to the art gallery that he owned with a business partner in Old Town Scottsdale where he was working for the summer. His business partner gave me a once over and teased us saying, "This must be the kisser." I grinned sheepishly and we left to have a lunch that would change the course of our lives.

That afternoon we sat on the patio of a colorful mid-century hotel's bar and he cut right to the chase of asking me a series of questions to test whether we were compatible. He'd been in two long-term relationships that didn't work out and was trepidatious after years of being on his own whether to try again. *Had I been in a romantic relationship before?* No. This was my first date. *Did I want children?* No. I was practically a child at the time. *What was I interested in sexually?* I had no idea. I'd never had sex with a man, but I knew that I wanted to try–preferably as soon as possible–so we paid the check, didn't bother returning to the gallery, and drove back to his home to find out.

There's nothing like the first time you're intimate with someone. That afternoon, I finally saw my fantasies come true of what it would be like to experience the taboo of stripping a man's clothes off and touching his skin. The magnetism feels like electricity running between your bodies as the arousal builds and all of the tension you've been holding onto is released. There's a truth revealed in their eyes when your gaze meets that's a secret to anyone else. And the truth for us both was that we'd been craving attention from someone who would reciprocate our affection for years. We were ravenous for love and that's what we found in each other.

My future husband took the rest of the week off so we could stay at home enjoying each other's company and getting to really know each other. We'd start the day with coffee while he read the newspaper, and I'd cook breakfast. Afternoons were spent poolside having deep conversations about religion and politics over bottomless gin and tonics. He wanted to know everything about being an officer in the military, and I wanted to learn everything about being a college professor. We immediately bonded over having competed in speech and debate, our passion for traveling, and love of the arts. We introduced each other to our favorite movies and music. Nesting in bed, we'd binge watch episodes of *Will & Grace* before nodding off together. It was the first time since grade school summers when I felt free of any responsibilities and truly happy. By the end of the week, we'd committed ourselves to each other like a couple having a shotgun wedding.

To celebrate, we planned our first trip together by touring the wineries of Napa and Sonoma. You don't fully know a person until you travel with them. In our relationship, he was the navigator and I was the driver, so we made a great team. His passion for art steered us toward museums and galleries while my obsession with restaurants became our guide. We were both planners, so our agenda was often obnoxious to anyone else who'd see our folders for every trip complete with Excel spreadsheets, but it worked for us. With glasses of wine in our hands looking out over the rows of grape vines lining the hills we could start to see our future. We were literally drunk in love.

After the trip, we started planning how to maintain a long-distance relationship with the restrictions of the military looming large. As my 60 days of leave came to an end, my husband drove with me to my first duty assignment at Goodfellow Air Force Base in San Angelo, Texas. We searched for apartments, and I introduced him as my uncle. This was the start of a series of fabrications to protect our relationship that took a heavy toll on my ethics, but I felt forced into making out of survival. I'd just received my Top Secret security clearance in order to start Intelligence training inside a Sensitive Compartmented Information Facility, and a paranoia set in that I'd somehow be caught, so we spent the majority of our time nesting in my apartment until my husband had to return to Phoenix. It was a tearful goodbye that would've been a farewell for most couples, but we committed to travel back and forth every few weeks to nurture what had quickly grown into a partnership.

Being stationed in a fairly remote part of West Texas proved to be the most challenging part of our arrangement because it required my driving three hours to Austin or Dallas to fly back to Phoenix, or six hours round trip for me to pick my husband up if he came to visit. The trips were normally only for two or three nights in as many weeks, so we always felt rushed. Compounded with my work schedule in the military, the routine grew exhausting and I began to doubt whether we could sustain such a schedule—not to mention the secrecy we needed to maintain. A part of me whispered on flights back home that maybe it would be healthier for us to return to our separate paths, but I never had the heart to initiate that conversation.

This was my first relationship, so I deferred to my Husband on what he recommended was best for us both rather than questioning his advice, and it led to an imbalance of power that reflected our 25 year difference in age. I was young and completely inexperienced with how to manage feelings of love in a rational way—not to mention developing my own identity as a gay man. We only had a small group of friends in Phoenix who knew we were a couple and never went to any gay bars. I can recall him saying there was no reason to associate with people at bars because, "They all want what we have," so he became my gatekeeper. We were living in a bubble that would inevitably pop.

It didn't help matters that so much of our day revolved around drinking double gin and tonics starting in the early afternoon. I'd always been a beer drinker who might have some with a meal or a whiskey on special occasions, but my husband's drink of choice was gin. Going to military school didn't allow regular drinking unless you were on leave, so I was more than familiar with the depression surrounding binge drinking, but I was never a daily drinker until our relationship began. Living alone away from my partner about whom no one could know about only made my drinking habits worse and caused me to gain 20 pounds over my usual weight of 150. My face grew puffy and my waistline expanded from the weight on my heart. I needed to either focus on my career or our relationship, so I made a decision to request reassignment to either Arizona or California so I could be closer to my husband.

In a great turn of fortune, my request was granted and I was given orders to report to Edwards Air Force Base in the desert north of Los Angeles. The change at least made the commute shorter to travel back and forth from Phoenix, but it was only a stop-gap solution. Leaving Intelligence decreased the anxiety of being caught violating the "Don't

Ask, Don't Tell" policy while holding a Top Secret security clearance, but transferring into the Services career field was a move that's often considered a way of putting an officer out to pasture. At this point, I'd accepted that my service in the military was only going to be for the short-term in order to fulfill the obligations of my commission, so we began to plan an exit strategy for me to begin graduate school after I completed my service.

Assigned to California in 2006, I embraced my roles as an Executive Officer, Flight Chief, and Officer in Charge of the Honor Guard. Unlike working in Intelligence, I felt like what I was doing made a difference and took pride in my work. I gradually made friends and was taken under the wing of senior leaders that I admired. It reminded me of being at the Air Force Academy and feeling a sense of duty, but there was still a part of me that was secret, disappearing for weekends to spend time with my partner. Living a double life simply wasn't emotionally sustainable, and weighed heavily on my ethics. When the economy took a downturn in 2007 and they began performing Reductions in Force (RIFs) in 2008, I took the unexpected opportunity to voluntarily separate from the military. It was the end of my career as a soldier and the beginning of a new chapter as an educator.

○ ○ ○

Leaving the Air Force allowed me to gradually begin to come out of the closet as a gay man to my family and friends. That fall, my husband and I attended the same conference where we had originally met in Chicago, but this time with the purpose of introducing him as my partner to my father. I had no idea how my Dad would react, so we arranged to meet in the lobby of the Palmer House hotel to avoid any overreaction, but thankfully it wasn't necessary. My father chuckled a little, clearly unsurprised, and warmly greeted my husband. We enjoyed a nice dinner breaking the ice and finished the evening with drinks at the hotel. The anxiety of what would happen on that trip plagued me for weeks leading up to the date, so it was a huge relief to be reminded that my father's love is unconditional.

The next challenge was coming out to my mother, and I wanted to show her the same respect as my father by telling her in person. Throughout my life, whenever I have something difficult to communicate to another person it's important to me that they can see my nonverbals that often communicate more than I can vocalize in moments of anxiety. Without the modern convenience of being able to have video calls with people, it took a toll on me as a child being limited to calling my mother over the phone and only seeing her in the summers. When I visited her, the tone was always positive and loving. She eventually gave birth to my two sisters, and our Mom raised us to be earnest, curious, and independent.

Her affection for children and good nature were traits that quietly yearned for grandchildren, and that's why I grew nervous about sharing that I wouldn't be able to have biological children; nor did we want to adopt. It was a matter of not wanting to disappoint a loved one who'd never actually communicated an expectation of me. In the opposite approach I took with my father, I chose to tell my mother in the car ride on the way to the airport where neither of us could avoid the moment once I shared the news. Her initial reaction was tearful, largely due to how hard she could tell it was for me to say the words out loud, but with the same knowingly unconditional support of me.

From that point on, it started to feel like one small battle after another each time it came to sharing my sexual identity and the complexity of being in a relationship with someone 25 years my senior. It feels like you're always coming out to someone new, and there's always an anxiety surrounding how people will react. I've had close friends and even family members stop talking to me, but I've also been overwhelmed by the majority of people who are unwavering allies. My husband and I were out in our personal lives, but neither of us were ever involved in many Pride events. We were certainly advocates in the classroom, but we never really became involved in the gay community, much less socialize with anyone outside of our professional networks.

In retrospect, there was an underlying sense of frustration that my growth as a gay man was pruned into a single branch by my partner and never given a chance to flourish. We both worked multiple jobs, regularly traveled, and enjoyed entertaining, so our schedule didn't leave much room for going to bars to socialize. In the course of our marriage, I can count on one hand the times we went to a gay bar, and when we did we'd just keep to ourselves. My husband's thinking was that going out was a waste of time since we already had each other, so I never experienced what it's like to make friends with men outside of work and learn much about gay culture. That part of me was exiled directly to jail without passing Go, and with every passing year my soul longed increasingly more for parole.

○ ○ ○

Being a student, coach, and teacher didn't leave a lot of time for tending to my marriage–much less to myself. While I was advancing through the stresses of establishing a professional identity, my husband was on the opposite side of his career transitioning into retirement. He wanted me home, and I wanted him to work, so neither of us was getting what we needed. Our interests were taking us in different directions that only overlapped in the evenings and mornings. We shared the same bed, but the longer we stayed together the less affectionate we became and the more we behaved like roommates stuck in a lease that couldn't be broken.

My small group of friends were scattered throughout the country, and the ones who lived locally were almost all raising children, so my social life was limited to my husband's menagerie of associates from the art world, academia, and his church—none of whom seemed to really care about me beyond polite conversation. The effect of essentially being a "kept man" was isolating, and I didn't feel that I had anyone to talk to about the challenges in my career and marriage. While I've always been able to reach out to my family for support, what I increasingly needed were people who shared the experience of what it's like to be gay in a largely heteronormative society—the sort of model that our relationship felt shoehorned into imitating.

It was important to my husband that everyone perceive that our marriage was just like any other *normal* pairing, and I followed that belief as someone who's always sought the approval of others. I was committed to finding ways for us to stay together because I didn't want our relationship to fail in the same way as my parents. After more than a decade, however, I began to question whether it was healthy for us to stay together if the main purpose was continuing to fall into the trap of keeping up with appearances. It was like we were forcing ourselves into the expected model of a traditional relationship, and that was no longer working for me. I questioned whether living with someone was the best situation for my mental and emotional state, always under the stress of tending to someone other than myself.

In the waning year of our marriage, working two full-time jobs kept me away from home more than ever, and perhaps staying so busy was a way of avoiding conversations that neither of us wanted to have. My husband needed my time and affection in the same way I needed my own space and independence. After nearly 15 years together, I was no longer willing to be deferential to my partner's preferences–much less remain quietly submissive to his choices without voicing my own perspective. My identity had been eclipsed by *our* identity as a couple. I found myself lost, feeling stuck in my marriage, and took that frustration out on my husband. Our home became a battleground for arguments and a place I started to avoid.

At the time, I was still working late hours at a restaurant. If it wasn't a particularly busy night they'd occasionally let us go home early, but I preferred staying out to steer clear of another conflict. Less than a mile away from the restaurant there was a run-down gay bar called Plazma that became a safe place for me just to have a drink and talk about my shift with the staff or fellow barflys. It's sad, but I felt better talking with strangers about the challenges I was facing instead of working through them with my own husband. We'd gone through some counseling sessions but stopped going when the therapist met with us separately and she told my husband that he needed to start planning for a life without me. It was advice we both chose to ignore discussing out of our codependence. Neither of us wanted to admit that our emotional distance was foreshadowing our eventual separation.

○ ○ ○

I left when I could no longer stay, and the people who came to my aid were surprisingly the ones who knew me the least: friends I'd met while chatting at Plazma. My husband's family and friends immediately excommunicated me, so the feeling of abandonment went both ways. I sought support from my immediate family, but my pride kept me from moving in with one of my parents or a relative. Instead, I accepted an offer to stay with a couple I'd recently met named Bill and Richie for a week while I searched for an apartment. Richie was a performer who hosted a drag show on Fridays, and his husband Bill would sit at the bar between setting up props and helping with costume changes.

After seeing the show a few times, I struck up a conversation with Bill and we became fast friends. I shared stories of the professional and personal problems I was trying to overcome, and he listened with empathy as someone who had faced similar challenges as a gay man. Bill and Richie gave me advice on how they'd gotten through difficult periods in their marriage, but by that point I'd already come to the conclusion that divorce was the only viable option for me.

Once I found a place of my own, there was a temptation to "crash out"–a phrase used to describe gay men who become overly social and promiscuous after repressing that side of their sexuality. In my case, the opportunity was short-lived as the onset of the pandemic coincided within weeks of my separation. On my own for the first time, I had a strong impulse to make up for the time I missed as a younger man to explore my identity prior to partnering with someone, but having to quarantine confined me to the metaphorical closet. The only people I had over to my apartment were Bill and Richie along with occasional visits from my Aunt when she brought over groceries. Meeting anyone in a bar or over the internet would have to wait until the eventual availability of the COVID vaccine, so the long period I'd gone through without affection only continued and kept me anchored in depression.

Once quarantine ended, Plazma re-opened and patrons gradually returned to the bar. The show on Fridays restarted and quickly became a day I reserved every week for fellowship with other gay men in a queer space like The Upstairs Lounge in New Orleans that Robert W. Fieseler referred to as a "Brotherhood of Men." Bill and Richie introduced me to their group of friends, and after spending the better part of a year on my own, I was eager to start rebuilding a social life–only this time I wanted my support system to be rooted within the gay community.

There was a part of me that was no longer willing to keep my identity in exile and wanted to make up for lost time, but after my divorce was finalized the last thing I wanted to do was fall back into what I viewed as the trappings of another relationship. I needed my independence as a means of protecting my heart from more trauma, so I grew emotionally distant from anyone who expressed an interest in dating. The phrase *No Strings Attached* became my middle name. I'd experienced what it's like to sacrifice one's happiness for another person's, and that's not the type of partnership I ever wanted to experience again.

After all of the hardships I've gone through, the characteristic that I drew the most strength from in recovering from my divorce was a contentment with being on my own. The period I spent bartending and living through the pandemic in isolation reminded me that the first person you need to help in a crisis is yourself. Knowing how close I came to drowning in a pool of depression, I finally realized the importance of embracing all the parts of my identity and the power that comes from making healthy decisions with them in mind. Taking time to enjoy my life is a choice that I plan to continue making.

○ ○ ○

It's been 3 years since my last shift bartending, and I'm grateful to be more content than I've ever been. After applying for countless job opportunities, I eventually found a consulting role with one of the largest banks in the world that engages me mentally and offers a level of financial security that working in hospitality could never provide. I still live in an apartment, but it's in a safer location and neighbors a gym that I go to on a daily basis to maintain my health. Most importantly, I'm surrounded by family and friends who love me unconditionally and are patient with the parts of me that remain a work in progress. Fridays are reserved for fellowship with my friends in the gay community who always make me smile and allow me to voice my anxieties as a form of social counseling. My heart is still mending, but I draw strength in living as a single man and find contentment in knowing that I don't need to find myself in another partner. However, I recently met someone who's made me reconsider the future.

During a trip to New York, I stopped by a gay bar that's like a time warp to the 70s with wood paneling and weathered carpet called the Townhouse. It was a crowded night for karaoke with men gathered around a piano singing showtunes. I made my way to the well to order a drink and while I was waiting, I noticed one of the most handsome men I've ever seen seated in the corner. My eyes lingered on him until he looked up and noticed me smiling. Unfortunately, he was in a conversation with a younger man who seemed to be isolating him, so I figured they were a couple and let him be; but to my surprise he gave me a subtle wink that made my heart start beating double-time. I nursed my drink from a distance until the younger man went to the bathroom and there was a window to briefly introduce myself–something I would have never had the courage to do years before. Out of all the gay men in a city of millions and thousands of miles from home, I knew that this was a rare opportunity, so I took the chance. It turned out the gentleman I'll call Jerry was just chatting to the younger man and single, visiting the city from Idaho on business, so I gave him my phone number hoping he shared the same interest. Up close, I melted for the soft features of his face, sterling hair, seafoam eyes, and wry smile. The younger man returned and Jerry winked at me again as he bid us goodnight and left the bar alone–a moment that kept me awake for half the night reliving.

The following afternoon, I received a call from a number I didn't recognize, so I figured it was a solicitor from a random number; letting the call ring until I suddenly realized that it might be Jerry and jerked to answer the phone. *Did I have time to meet up for lunch?* My heart started beating double-time again. It was the final day of my trip, and I was planning to go to one of my favorite restaurants that's inside the Museum of Modern Art, so I extended an invitation. Following my divorce, I socialized with gay men and periodically had fun with the ones who piqued my interest, but I couldn't recall going on an actual date since the first time I met my former husband.

That afternoon was like going back 20 years to the same moment, but with different eyes. Conversation poured out of us like two people thirsty for getting to know each other. It turned out his father was a Marine and his mother worked in education, so we quickly bonded over those intersections. Jerry worked in real estate and loved to travel, so we shared a number of professional and personal goals. Most importantly, there was an immediate connection between us that was building tension. *What was I doing for the rest of the afternoon?* A devilish grin crossed my face that he thankfully returned, so we paid the check and walked to his hotel.

The room had a stunning view of Central Park, but all I wanted to see was more of Jerry. Having sex with someone can be a completely physical act, but when we touched there was a tenderness I hadn't experienced in a long time. As we kissed, I could feel his gaze on me, and when I looked deep into his eyes it was like diving into a pool. There was an awkwardness and excitement that felt like making love for the first time. I was bracing for him not to feel the same passion and go our separate ways like so many hook-ups end, but Jerry surprised me with another question: *What was I doing for the rest of the day?*

My idea of a perfect day starts with waking up in a place like New York while traveling where there are endless possibilities, taking a morning walk to find a local coffee shop, enjoying a leisurely lunch, touring cultural landmarks like museums, going to happy hour at a gay bar, and finally meeting someone easy on the eyes who can hold a thoughtful conversation over a memorable dinner. That afternoon, Jerry and I went to the Whitney Museum for their Biennial exhibition, hopped around the bars near Stonewall, and went to his favorite Italian restaurant. In the matter of 24 hours, we went from strangers into fellow travelers holding hands under the dinner table. We returned to his hotel for a night cap where there was an opportunity for us to sleep together, but my flight home was scheduled in the morning, so I asked him to promise that we would see each other again and he kindly agreed. Walking back to where I was staying, scenarios of spending more time with Jerry swirled in my mind and I realized how similar the day—one of the happiest of my life—was to when I met my former husband.

Waiting on the tarmac for my flight home to take off the following morning, I thought about all the love and effort that went into building my former marriage. The flights back and forth every other week to maintain a long-distance relationship for years, and the lengths we went to in order to protect our love from the bigotry of the military at the time. Ultimately, the good years outnumbered the challenging ones, so I hope that my former husband will find another partner who can provide all the happiness he deserves.

As for me, *Have I healed enough to try again?* For the first time in over a decade, I've been singing love songs to myself that I hear on the radio, and daydreaming about waking up next to someone who makes my heart beat a little faster just for him. I'm starting to think I might be ready for another round with a man who makes me smile like Jerry, but this time as the self I found on the other side of hardship, and not the person who nearly sacrificed everything by tending to others first. Change takes time and requires sustained effort, but if you're patient with yourself and embrace the support of your community then there's nothing you can't recover from.

CHAPTER 10

THE BARTENDER

Finally, a chapter on bartending. During my time working in fine dining, I ran a beverage program that encompassed knowledge of every type of product derived from fermentation or distilling for pairing with the restaurant's menu. That experience led to roles bartending at four different types of establishments: a brewery, wine bistro, dive, and gay bar. In order, I was the most knowledgeable about beer, least proficient with wine, depressed by hitting bottom, and happy to serve my community. Being a bartender took every part of my personality because the type of work and clientele varied wildly between jobs. The brewery required me to be knowledgeable about the entire fermentation process and the differences between all the different styles of beer, so I was fortunate to have all the experience of working with my father. Conversely, the wine bistro demanded proper etiquette for bottle service and a mind-boggling vocabulary that I simply hadn't taken enough time to study, so it challenged me to learn as much as I could on a daily basis. The dive bar served a combination of lower quality beer, wine, and limited alcohol selections that I found frustrating to represent–much less recommend–to guests. Finally, the gay bar had a vast number of spirits that could've potentially been made into hundreds of different cocktails, but it was amusing how nearly 80% of the orders were vodka sodas or gin and tonics. Each role was a learning opportunity when it came to the amount of labor that goes into the seemingly simple task of pouring liquid from one vessel into another and transporting it in a glass to a patron only a few feet away.

Due to the misconception that serving drinks is a job that anyone could perform, the majority of society looks down on the profession of bartending. In turn, the purpose of sharing my stories is to humanize working in the industry for individuals who are often treated with condescension, so I hope that each time you order a drink, you realize that the person on the other side of the bar has their own challenging experiences like myself they're struggling with. Between the long hours on your feet without breaks and bare minimum wages, I can guarantee that most readers wouldn't last a week bartending. It's a trade that's always in demand and knows there will perpetually be someone in need of a job, so there's a level of exploitation in the industry that feeds a culture of cynicism.

One of the first things they told me in bartending is that it should never be your full-time, or only, gig. Unless you're involved in some level of ownership or happen into the rare role of a salaried position, bartending will never change from being a minimum-wage, entry-level, position with high turnover. You can get in an argument with management and leave the job at the drop of a hat. Days later you can be working in a new bar. It's a trade that's always in demand because few people can tolerate the work. The only thing secure about bartending is it'll be there for you when nothing else is available.

Most of us are on a spectrum from those who take pride in their work to those who don't give a fuck. The latter is the only way to endure a career in the service industry. "Dead inside" as a former manager used to say. While I took pride in being efficient and knowledgeable, the truth is that I was far too sensitive to be behind the bar long-term. I'm proud that I lasted as long as I did, but the interactions with guests I viewed as disrespectful or abusive grated on my nerves. You learn a lot about people by the way they treat you, and while I believe the average patron is a decent human being, there are assholes who love asserting their power over those who find themselves in service roles. In turn, the most important lesson I took away from my experience was building empathy for my fellow bartenders. Saying hello, ordering politely, showing thanks, being mindful of other guests, leaving a tip, and pushing your chair in when you leave are all behaviors that go a long way toward helping a bartender get through their day, so this final chapter is designed to share my unsolicited advice from my experiences on simple ways to show your mindfulness.

Opening

Bartending is about the constant maintenance of a given space, products, and clientele. Every shift requires cleaning, stocking, and preparing to welcome guests by following checklists accounting for all the tasks to accomplish before ever opening the doors. For me, there was a certain zen to being left alone to crank up the volume on the music and get to work. Each day starts by filling the mop bucket and tracing the same pattern around the bar. While the floor dries, the next task is stocking any items that are running low or out from the night before. The placement of bottles often gets disorganized between different bartenders and their styles, so going through the inventory is an opportunity to make sure everything is in its right place and where you need it to be when a shift gets busy. Once the floor dries, it's time to arrange the chairs, make sure the bathrooms are squared away, all the lights are dialed to the right setting, and the electronics are up and running. Ideally, you want the place to be presentable and welcoming like you would in your home. The floors should be void of debris, counters polished, menu updated, deliveries sorted, and ready to open on time. Then it's time to cue up the music and turn on any televisions before unlocking the door and letting the next shift begin.

Atmosphere

One of a bartender's greatest powers is controlling the atmosphere created by the style and volume of music as well as the mood of the lighting. Unfortunately, managers tend to keep a tight reign on these aspects of the business. For example, the brewery always required us to play *Black Keys* radio that quickly grew annoyingly repetitive just like the bistro insisted on recycling the same instrumental tracks every night. The brewery also emphasized opening up the rolling garage doors to let in as much natural light as we could to attract more families, while the gay bar was a windowless space that was always dimmed to be more forgiving on guests' appearance. Managers usually have a reason for why they want things set a certain way that's understandable, but having strict policies doesn't allow bartenders to adapt to the sort of crowd that's in the space. The dive bar was the only place that gave me the license to make my own decisions, so I took a certain pride whenever someone would compliment a playlist or how I'd adjust the lights depending on the time of day. Little touches can go a long way to making people feel comfortable, so it's also important to keep your audience in mind as well as adapt when a guest makes a request.

When I was working at the wine bistro there was an elderly woman with hearing aids who repeatedly asked me to turn down the volume of the music, but each time I relayed the message to the owner he refused without reason, making her feel so ignored that she expressed that they would never return. In contrast, when I would notice that the composition of the crowd at the dive bar was mainly couples, I'd adjust the music to play more love songs, steer their orders toward sharing a bottle of wine, turn off the televisions, and dim the lighting. I know it sounds a little eye-roll inducing, but two of our regulars who started dating while I worked there later got married and had a child, which might not have happened if the atmosphere hadn't been adaptable.

Greetings

An attentive bartender always keeps an eye out on the entrance. While the consideration of security plays a role in sizing up whoever walks through the door, the main reason is to greet guests when they enter. It can be a simple wave, eye-contact with a smile, or a phrase like "Welcome in" that signals you'll be with them as soon as you can. Few things frustrate me more than being ignored when you're paying for a service, so it was important to me that everyone feel acknowledged without waiting too long. Once we get to you, the interaction should follow a generic script:

Hi there. How can I help?

Hello. I'll have a glass of Chardonnay please.

Sounds good. I'll be right back.

Thanks.

Unfortunately, this seemingly basic exchange represents a small number of interactions. I know I'm in the minority, but manners matter. When greeted with a warm welcome and respect, it goes a long way if you can reciprocate. Avoiding eye contact, ignoring pleasantries, and ordering with condescension mean that you'll be receiving bare minimum service. If I had to choose between being treated with respect or being thanked, I'll always choose the former. Just because a person is working behind a bar doesn't mean they're less worthy of common decency.

Water

In a restaurant setting, it's common practice to start by serving the table with water and potentially asking what type, but this proves wasteful in most bar settings because the simple majority of guests never touch it. When you assume everyone wants water, you typically end up pouring it down the sink and creating another glass to clean, so by the time I ended working in a dive bar I simply stopped asking. My thinking on the subject, particularly living in the Arizona desert, is that if you want water then ask for it. Please don't be the person who orders a glass of water and when we return ask for club soda instead and when we return *again* ask for it without ice and when we return *yet again* ask for a lemon. If you're that demanding then at least let us know up front, so we can avoid you. The main exception is if someone orders three or more drinks and needs to hydrate then I'll set a glass in front of them as a subtle signal to slow down if they're driving. After all, we're here to help take care of you and make sure we'll see you again soon.

Ordering

Want to know how to order a drink without sounding like an asshole? Start with the knowledge that there are (usually) other people in the bar that were there before you. We're serving them currently and will be with you shortly. Notice when bartenders sometimes walk by you without making eye contact? It's because we don't have an immediate moment, and we're usually trying to remember an order, so when we get interrupted that's when we start to make mistakes. However, a good bartender doesn't avert their eyes. Instead, they make eye contact and either say or motion that they'll be with you shortly. Once this happens, please be patient. You aren't going to die of thirst. Also, remember to be cognizant of your demeanor and tone. Why start our interaction with being pissed off and demanding? Again, the way you greet people immediately communicates the type of interaction we're going to have and the sort of personality you are, so try to start on a positive note. This goes both ways. Guests should be greeted in a welcoming fashion and have their questions patiently answered. We're always happy to steer you towards a drink and often provide samples. As adults, our primary hope is that you know what you like instead of asking us–complete strangers–to guess what you might enjoy. Your order is a reflection of yourself.

Appearance

Having a uniform was something that I considered in each establishment I worked in. I wore a suit and tie in fine dining, company branded shirts in the brewery, a button-up shirt with suspenders in the wine bistro, shorts and a hoodie in the dive, and snug jeans with a tight-fitting shirt in the gay bar. The idea was to reflect the atmosphere the business was trying to capture before ever speaking to a guest. When I used to teach Nonverbal Communication, an emphasis of the course was getting students to realize how everything about your appearance can contribute to being read (or judged) by another person. While age, gender, and race are prominent examples, choices in how you present yourself like hairstyle, grooming, tattoos, piercings, and weight also subtly serve as clues to your personality. In my case, going to work has always come with some version of a dress code for playing a role. For example, in the military it was an actual uniform with a high and tight haircut, and in the classroom it was a tie and blazer with longer hair. Each served a purpose in communicating before speaking. I wanted people to readily identify who I was and my purpose in the setting whether to lead, serve, teach, wait, or tend. For better or worse, it works the opposite way, too. Bartenders notice how you present yourself and it helps us size up how to approach you or what we might have to deal with.

Seating

Given the choice of sitting at a table or a bar, I'll always choose sitting closer to the action. It's the easiest way to get a drink if there's only one or two people working rather than waiting for someone to leave the bar unattended to go to your table. It's also important for bartenders to keep the seating orderly and welcoming. As a person that's often on my own when I'm off work, I advocate for keeping an odd number of stools at the bar so it's not always designed for couples. Want faster service? Go to the well or register. Want to have a conversation? Belly up to the bar. Want to meet someone? Take a chance and start a conversation with the person next to you. Your experience will be dictated by your choices, and it's our job to provide you with the best options. Want to show an act of kindness on your way out? We'll always appreciate it if you push your chair back into the position you found it in.

Bathrooms

Maintaining a presentable bathroom is much more difficult than you think. In fine dining, we were expected to tidy the facilities after each use, but that's impossible while bartending by yourself, so it's essential that everything be stocked at the beginning of a shift. On top of cleaning all the surfaces, you have to ensure the soap is filled, provide extra toilet paper, and add paper towels (if you don't have a hand dryer). Over the course of the evening, all of those items will be diminished. The trash can will be overflowing; piss will collect on the floor around the toilet, and the sink area will be splattered with soap and water along with a lottery of detritus. The worst case scenarios are if there's a plumbing problem or someone throws up in the middle of service. Unfortunately, I've had to clean up all varieties of the latter from the floor and walls to a urinal or sink (which is the grossest possible option). Imagine putting on gloves to pick brown chunks out of a filter while holding back the urge to vomit from the stench. It's disgusting and degrading. The toilet exists for disposing of a variety of reasons, so please maximize its potential. Uncomfortable with gender neutral bathrooms? Get over it. I can assure you that there isn't a singular gender that trashes or maintains tidier restrooms. It comes down to the person and how considerate they are of shared public spaces.

Side Work

In addition to maintaining bathrooms, perpetually sanitizing surfaces, sweeping the floor, refilling ice, keeping bottles organized, and cleaning glasses are all examples of what's called side work. While serving drinks is your primary job, doing so inherently creates additional tasks that stack up; especially if you're working alone. There's a spectrum of bartenders who range from those who stay on top of side work to the ones who neglect it and pass it on to the next person's shift. I tried my best to be the former with an eye for details like spotting and throwing out any chipped glasses. When you learn how to pay attention, you become conditioned to notice everything even when you're not working. In turn, the experience of what it's like to go to a bar on your day off forever changes. Knowing the effort it takes, you begin to truly appreciate great service, but also grow critical of lackluster efforts. *What's the biggest sign of a bartender's value?* Whether they're doing side work like clearing tables and sanitizing surfaces between tasks. *Want to lend a helping hand on your way out if you're seated away from the bar?* Please dispose of any trash you bring in rather than leaving it on the table and bring your glasses back to the counter you're able. We'll always appreciate having one less task to perform on the side.

Conversation

A good bartender listens rather than gives advice. After all, I ended up here and you're on the other side of the bar, so we've clearly made different life choices. Beyond pleasantries when ordering, most couples or groups of friends aren't seeking to make small talk, but people on their own typically like to have a bit of conversation. This is where having some interpersonal skills and trivial knowledge comes in handy. Beyond talking about the different items you serve, it goes a long way to getting a patron to stay and have another round or two if you're able to engage them about what's going on in topics like sports or popular culture. Keeping the subject neutral helps prevent clashes about politics or religion. There's a happy medium to balance between avoiding a conversation and being so engrossed that you neglect other guests. In general, monopolizing a bartender's time creates back-ups and impacts everyone around you, so try and exercise some self-awareness of your wants compared to other guests. However, it's also an important responsibility on the part of a bartender to recognize when a guest could really use the support of someone to simply listen with empathy.

There's one conversation that stands out when working at the dive bar that I'll never forget. It was dead on a weekday approaching midnight with no one in the bar, so I was killing time until closing by watching The *Lord of the Rings* on the small television by the glass front door where I could see anyone approaching. Usually I'd notice whenever a car would drive up and park, but I was surprised by a well-groomed man around 30 years old with a black leather jacket, who must've been a pedestrian. He walked in and took a seat near the register. He ordered a lager and when I returned he asked me if I knew the owner of a neighboring bar by name. "Not really," I replied. He took out his wallet and set a $100 bill on the counter. *Are you sure?*

As much as that money would've doubled what I made that shift, I'd honestly never met who he was asking about, so I shrugged my shoulders and apologized. I never could've predicted what came out of his mouth next. "I'm going to kill him." The words blindsided me, so I tried to diffuse the intensity of the moment by asking, "Whoa, man! What did this guy do?" *That motherfucker kicked me out!* I could guess the reason but kept that sarcastic comment to myself. "What happened?" I tried to keep him talking to avoid the silence, but he avoided answering and ordered another lager. When I got back, he took out his wallet again, put another $100 bill on the counter, and returned to his original question: *Are you sure you don't know this guy?* This time adding, *Where can I find him?* with the implication that if I helped him stalk the owner then the money was mine. *I'm going to kill him!* he repeated as he raised his shoulder enough to show me the holstered handgun in his jacket.

"Hey, man. I'm sorry this asshole kicked you out," I said trying to deescalate the situation, "but I really don't know anything about him." There was no amount of money that would make me choose to become an accomplice to what he was threatening, but he must've sensed that the bills on the table were tempting, so he took out yet another $100 and stacked it on top of the others. *Tell me where I can find this guy and the cash is yours.* He studied my face like a card player weighing whether someone is bluffing. *You're sure you don't know this guy, huh?* I apologized again and he seemed convinced enough to polish off the rest of his beer rather than continue the conversation. *I'm going to kill him!* he emphasized as he rose to leave and disappeared into the night.

As soon as he was gone, I looked up the number for the bar in question and called to warn them of the threat and possibility that the man was walking there next, but the manager just chuckled. "We hear stuff like that all the time," he replied before abruptly ending the conversation. Left dumbfounded and with my heart racing, I considered whether I'd done the right thing or needed to call the police. I decided that my description and the security footage could readily identify the man if any violence was committed then went about my business closing the bar. That's when I noticed that he'd left the three crisp bills on the counter, stuffed them in my pocket as a tip, and locked the door.

Tipping

Tipping is a way of acknowledging that the profession of hospitality isn't compensated enough and far from sustainable. Tips from regulars are what we rely on and we're always cynical about one-time customers who are abusive because they know they'll never come back. All forms of tipping help to some degree, but cash is always king. Honestly, the funds basically get passed on to other industry workers by us buying drinks at other bars because we know that's the best form of appreciation. People love to use the term "I appreciate you" these days, but that's very different from being valued. We're working a grinding job to get paid, not fishing for compliments or seeking condescending advice scrawled at the bottom of a receipt rationalizing not leaving a tip. That sort of behavior will get you chased out the front door and shared on social media after we've realized what you've done.

My poorest response to this type of act happened at the wine bar one evening after listening to a French-Canadian man in his 50s with the face of Arthur Slugworth who was clearly on an outing with a young female escort. With the arrival of each course, he would try to demonstrate his knowledge of wine and cuisine to her by trying to stump me with questions, which I quickly grew exhausted by and eventually didn't have an answer. He was one of the rudest people I've ever met in the dining context, and at the end of the meal he took out his phone and opened the calculator application. After he punched in the numbers, he signed the check and they quickly exited. Later, when we were processing receipts I realized that his calculation was to tip 15% off of the meal only (excluding the bottle service) and before tax. Taking my own calculator out, the difference was roughly $40 instead of $100–and I can assure you I needed that $60 a lot more than this asshole.

Then a rare opportunity presented itself: The man had made a reservation with another woman for the next night. Visions of revenge immediately flooded my thoughts. *What could I do to teach this guy a lesson?* I could've easily performed some sort of disgusting act, but that's never been my style. When I notice injustice, I do my best to confront it, so through the entire service I stalked like a lion in the long grass waiting for the right moment to pounce and give him a piece of my mind on behalf of all of the workers in the service industry he'd cheated over the decades–not to mention on the woman who turned out to be his wife. At the time, the minimum wage in Arizona was $12 per hour and the common practice was to tip 20% on the total bill (which we get taxed on), so I settled on emphasizing this as my message. The same pattern from the night before repeated itself with questions during the presentation of each course and overhearing his nauseating one-sided conversation gloating about his affluence I'd overhear when clearing dishes and glassware. This was a worldly person who wasn't new to American custom, he was simply an abusive personality and terrible guest.

As the meal drew to a close, he raised his hand to beckon for the bill and snapped his fingers with a sound that made me want to do the same to his neck. Now was the time. I printed the tab, placed it in the bill holder, and returned to the table. He reached for it and I maintained my grip. I had a tip for him. "Are you aware of what the minimum wage is that we work for?" He shrugged. "It's $12 an hour, so we can only make a living in this profession through tips that are normally 20%" Knowing his wife likely didn't realize he was in the night before, I continued, "When you were in last evening, I noticed you left 15% and didn't include the bottle service. This time, I hope you'll do the right thing so I can have a meal for myself that's a fraction of what you've just experienced." Mic drop. His wife's face was mortified, and as I turned my back to make my way back to the kitchen I noticed that the rest of the tables were watching. My emotions had gotten the better of me, but it was an exorcism from the wine bistro I needed to perform. When I returned from the kitchen to tend to another table, I noticed that the couple had quickly exited–thankfully leaving a 20% tip.

86ed

When a bartender cuts you off and stops serving you drinks, we're trying to help keep you from making drunken mistakes as well as, hopefully, ensure you get home safely. Being 86ed, or told never to return, means that you're beyond our help. There's a distinct difference. Dealing with drunk people is a core function of our profession, so it becomes second nature to notice when someone's face reddens, their eyes grow watery, and they have trouble focusing–not to mention the loss of motor function. As a general rule, I've found that after three drinks the alcohol begins to hit a person's system and we start seeing the signs. We won't necessarily cut you off at that point, but a good bartender will pour you a glass of water and check if you have a ride home. Fortunately, we live in an incredible moment in history where ride-sharing services and even autonomous-driving cars are available to help you (and us) from getting into trouble. No one wants you getting a DUI, particularly if the police want to hold the bar responsible for over-serving you.

In my three years of bartending, I cut people off plenty of times, but only 86ed one customer. It was a busy Friday night at the dive bar when two African-American women in their 20s entered that I'd never met before, so I greeted them as they sat down by introducing myself. "Okay, *Nick*" one said, emphasizing my name. "I just flew in from Dallas and need a double vodka on the rocks." Red flag #1. Her friend looked a little embarrassed like she may have been in before and knew this already. "Unfortunately, we only have a beer and wine license," I replied. "Is there any style of those you might like?" The traveler let out an exhausted sigh. "Really, *Nick*?! What kind of place is this, *Nick*?!" Our menu was fairly extensive and written on the wall in chalk. She took a cursory look and said, "What's the strongest thing you've got, *Nick*?" Red flag #2. While the way she was purposefully saying my name at the end of every sentence like someone working in sales was quickly growing annoying, she didn't show any signs of being drunk, so I suggested a triple IPA style beer that was 12% alcohol. She replied, "Fine, *Nick*," and her friend quietly ordered a cider. I returned a few moments later with their drinks and the traveler piped up, "We're gonna take care of you, *Nick*, so keep 'em coming." Red flag #3. Anyone who says they're going to take care of you is going to assuredly cheat you on your tip, so I was braced for how things were likely going to end up.

I left to attend to other guests and a few moments later I heard the traveler's voice calling me in a volume the entire bar could hear. "We're empty, *Nick*!" The guests I was serving gave me a look like they could tell things were getting a little awkward. I could see that the traveler had clearly chugged her beer. Red flag #4. Her friend had barely touched her cider and remained quiet. Rather than suggest she slow down, I poured the traveler another glass figuring she must've had a rough day. "Thank you, *Nick*. We're going to take care of you," she repeated. "I appreciate that," I replied and managed a smile before leaving to attend to other guests, but it wasn't five minutes before she beckoned me again. "We're empty, *Nick*!"

By this point the traveler had become a distraction for everyone in the bar, so I returned with a glass of water and suggested she take things a little more slowly. "Don't you dare tell me what to do, *Nick*!" she sneered. Red flag #5. Her friend turned and tried to get the traveler to calm down, but that only agitated her more. "No, fuck that! We're empty, *Nick*!" she repeated while staring me down. Then came the unexpected. I was wearing a shirt from a brewery in Flagstaff called Dark Sky with their logo in a rainbow for Pride. Her focus drifted from my eyes down to study the shirt. "*Dark Sky*, huh, *Nick*?" she asked. "That sounds like some racist shit. I'll bet you're a racist, *Nick*!" Red flag #6. I was completely stupefied by her accusation. "It's just a brewery in Flagstaff," I tried to defend myself, but a card had been played that couldn't be returned to the deck. "You're not serving me because I'm black, huh, *Nick*?!" The entire bar was watching and the tension was palpable. I was at a loss for how to respond, so rather than escalate the argument, I caved out of embarrassment and poured her another beer as a form of pacification.

I left to attend to the other guests and everyone I served asked me a version of "What's going on?" I shrugged and tried to continue working while I kept watching the traveler out of the corner of my eye. She and her friend were clearly having a disagreement and I was hoping that she might convince the traveler to leave, but then the words returned, "No, fuck that! We're empty, *Nick*!" In response, her friend stood up and began to take out her purse to pay, so I quickly returned with the tab to help facilitate a quick exit, but the traveler was painfully intent on staying. "You're not serving me because I'm black, huh, *Nick*?!" I'd made the mistake of allowing her to bully me with this statement before, so it was time for a different approach. I took out my phone to video record the scene and said, "Look, I'm sorry you feel that way, but you've had too many tonight and I need to cut you off." As the video started recording, her friend left cash on the table and walked toward the exit while the traveler covered her face. "Fuck you, *Nick*! You racist mother fucker!" Then she snatched the money from the bar and stomped away.

Through the glass front door, I could see that her friend was in the driver's seat of a Jeep waiting to leave, but the traveler refused to get in on the passenger side. She was furious and the obscenities were so loud we could still hear them inside as she started pounding her fists on the driver's side glass for her friend to give her the keys. After about a minute of this, her friend relented, opened the Jeep's door, and gave the traveler her keys. Then, as the friend started to walk to the other side of the Jeep, the traveler started the ignition and punched the gas as fast as she could in reverse–leaving her friend in the smoke of the rubber from the Jeep's peeling out. The thought that I was responsible for over-serving her flashed into my mind as you could hear the engine rev and the traveler sped out of the parking lot. A horn blared from another car as she careened onto the street and I was filled with the dread that she was going to kill someone on the road, but fortunately there wasn't an accident–at least not that we were ever notified about later.

The friend remained outside and slumped down on the curb, so I left the bar for a moment to see if she was okay and needed help calling a ride. "I'm so sorry about my friend," she said. It was the first time I'd heard her speak since she ordered a cider. The thought occurred to me that this likely wasn't the first time this had happened, so I started to feel bad for her situation. "Do you need me to call a ride service for you?" I asked. "That's okay. I can do it on my phone" she managed. "You're more than welcome to wait inside," I encouraged her, but she shook her head no, so I returned to the bar. To my surprise, the guests who had all been watching erupted in applause like it was my birthday. With order restored, I went about my business and kept an eye on the friend until a car arrived for her. As they drove away, I suddenly realized they hadn't paid, but I figured it was worth the cost just to have the ordeal over with. Of course, they hadn't taken care of me with a tip, but that's the sort of treatment you get from someone who deserves to be 86ed.

Closing

After the last call for drinks passes and customers gradually filter out, it's time to start closing down the bar. You lock the door, dim the lights, and try to perform all the tasks on the checklist as quickly as possible so you can go home at a decent hour. Each of the settings I worked in were slightly different, but the pattern is generally the same. Surfaces come first so all the glasses are collected from tables and any debris on the bar is wiped onto the floor. Next, you flip all the chairs to rest on the tables and bar to clear space for sweeping. You find yourself moving in a circular pattern around the bar completing a new task with each pass like being inside the gears of a clock. Once the space is sanitized, it's time to process the credit card payments and count the register, ensuring the number matches the total in sales. Some might say that stocking and mopping should also be part of closing, but the fact is that the later shift is always busier and you're exhausted at the end of the night, so it's a duty that's generally passed on to the person opening the next day.

In exchange, the last responsibility of closing before you lock the doors is potentially the most dangerous part of the job: taking out the trash. *Why?* Public dumpsters offer a convenient place to take drugs in a relatively secluded location as well as easily dispose of paraphernalia, so addicts notoriously hover around bins like bees protecting their hive. Disturbing them puts you at risk of being stung, so keeping a cautionary eye out for their buzzing around the bins becomes part of the job. The dumpster in the alley of the dive bar was particularly attractive to junkies and homeless people roaming the midtown neighborhood to the point where I can remember it being pointed out during my orientation shift as a potential hazard we needed to monitor. Sure enough, I encountered two junkies near the dumpster while closing during my first week, so I left the trash bags near the back door for the person opening hoping that the light of day would ward them away. However, after you've observed people on drugs long enough you realize that the time of day has little to do with satisfying cravings. Hungry people don't just eat dinner; nor do addicts only get their fix at night.

Towards the end of my time bartending, there was a closing shift I covered and when I went to take out the garbage and discovered an older woman with disheveled hair lying face down on the ground near the bin as if she'd been discarded with the rest of the trash. While I paused for a moment to consider what to do, a teenage boy on a bike rode by in front of me and commented, "That lady's dead!" *What fresh hell is this?* I thought to myself, knowing that the right thing to do in the situation was to check on her. She was frozen with no sign of breathing, so I made my way up to her to check for a pulse. Then, as my hand drew close to her neck, she suddenly jolted back to life with a gasp like the scene where Uma Thurman is resuscitated from a drug overdose by a needle injection to her heart in *Pulp Fiction*. The incident scared the hell out of me, and I couldn't shake thinking about it for months.

There were many days during my time bartending when I felt like trash who'd been discarded. More specifically, that I'd thrown away my future by falling into the sort of slippery slope I imagined the woman by the dumpster had made. Maybe she had a career that was derailed like mine. Maybe she had a partner who she no longer felt safe with, too. Maybe she found herself working in a dead-end profession because there were no other prospects. Maybe that job required the sort of physical labor that led her to start taking drugs. Maybe her addiction led to losing her dead-end job. Maybe being out of work caused her to be evicted. Maybe losing her home was a shame she felt she could never recover from and addiction became her only escape from hopelessness. Maybe she had surrendered to the idea that dying face down by a dumpster was a fitting end to her story, but I refused for that to be mine.

o o o

The story of my three years bartending thankfully ended with a new beginning, so the message of this book is for anyone recovering from setbacks in their lives that could use a reminder to never give up on yourself and hold on to the hope that tomorrow offers if you can have the patience to take each day at a time. I also hope that sharing my experience of working in the service industry will provide readers on the other side of the bar with a more empathic perspective if you consider that every bartender has stories like my own. Recovering from the loss of my career and marriage challenged me with finding a way to rebuild my life that took realizing that I needed to tend to my own needs before I could be attentive to others. I learned what it takes to get out of bed every morning and keep trying to heal:

The courage to admit you have problems;

the strength to distance from codependency;

the willingness to let go of the past;

the humility to accept help from others;

the determination to find a place of security;

the introspection to let go of destructive patterns;

the dedication to maintain your physical health;

the commitment to nurture your relationships;

the authenticity to embrace your community;

and the compassion to serve others with dignity.

EPILOGUE

CLINIC OUTTAKE FORM

9 February 2023

Are you currently having any of the following problems?

Feelings of depression?   [No]

Loss of interest in activities?   [No]

Feeling hopeless?   [No]

Problems going to sleep?   [No]

Racing thoughts?   [No]

Acting impulsively?   [No]

Worrying excessively?   [No]

Feeling worthless?   [No]

Traumas that come back in nightmares?   [No]

Feeling awkward in public?   [Yes]

Having tense muscles?   [No]

Repetitive or compulsive behaviors?   [Yes]

Thoughts that replay?   [Yes]

Eating too little?   [No]

Concerns about alcohol use?   [Yes]

Problems caring for yourself?   [No]

Thoughts of not being alive?   [No]

RECOMMENDATIONS

The National Suicide Prevention Hotline: Dial 988

Codependent No More
> Melody Beattie, Spiegel & Grau, 2022.

No Bad Parts
> Dr. Richard C. Schwartz, Sounds True, 2021.

Mindset: The New Psychology of Success
> Dr. Carol Dweck, Ballantine, 2006.

Deep & Simple: A Spiritual Path for Modern Times
> Bo Lozoff, Human Kindness Foundation, 1999.

A Room of One's Own
> Virginia Woolf, Harcourt, 1929.

THREE YEARS IN TENDING

A MEMOIR

Nicholas D. Butler